WORLD WAR I FOR KIDS

Everything You Need to Know - Amazing Facts, Heroic Acts, Major Battles, and How the War Changed the World

James Burrows

© Copyright 2024 - All rights reserved.

The content contained within this book may not be reproduced, duplicated or transmitted without direct written permission from the author or the publisher.

Under no circumstances will any blame or legal responsibility be held against the publisher, or author, for any damages, reparation, or monetary loss due to the information contained within this book, either directly or indirectly.

Legal Notice:

This book is copyright protected. It is only for personal use. You cannot amend, distribute, sell, use, quote or paraphrase any part, or the content within this book, without the consent of the author or publisher.

Disclaimer Notice:

Please note the information contained within this document is for educational and entertainment purposes only. All effort has been executed to present accurate, up to date, reliable, complete information. No warranties of any kind are declared or implied. Readers acknowledge that the author is not engaged in the rendering of legal, financial, medical or professional advice. The content within this book has been derived from various sources. Please consult a licensed professional before attempting any techniques outlined in this book.

By reading this document, the reader agrees that under no circumstances is the author responsible for any losses, direct or indirect, that are incurred as a result of the use of the information contained within this document, including, but not limited to, errors, omissions, or inaccuracies.

Other Books by James Burrows

What You Need To Know:

World War I for Teens
World War I for Kids
World War II for Teens
World War II for Kids

The Ultimate Guide:

Egyptian Mythology for Kids
Greek Mythology for Kids
Norse Mythology for Kids

Other Books:

The Art of War – Sun Tzu
Mediations – Marcus Aurelius

A NOTE FOR PARENTS

I hope your children enjoy this book. I've included this note to highlight that whilst I have not included some of the worst aspects of World War 1, it still includes descriptions of battles, injuries, and hardships that you may want to check first, especially for younger readers.

I'm sure children will enjoy finding out about this significant event in history, but you may want to read it with them, or at least be prepared for any questions they may have.

CONTENTS

1. WELCOME TO THE BATTLEFIELD

2. TIMELINE OF THE WAR

3. WHAT CAUSED WORLD WAR 1

4. WHICH COUNTRIES TOOK PART

5. WORLD WAR 1 IN NUMBERS

6. TACTICS AND TECHNOLOGY

7. LEADERS AND GENERALS

8. 1914 - MAJOR EVENTS & BATTLES

9. 1915 - MAJOR EVENTS & BATTLES

10. 1916 - MAJOR EVENTS & BATTLES

11. 1917 - MAJOR EVENTS & BATTLES

12. 1918 - MAJOR EVENTS & BATTLES HOW THE WAR ENDED

13. LIFE IN THE TRENCHES

14. WW1 HEROES

15. HOW THE WAR CHANGED THE WORLD

16. CONCLUSION

ABOUT THE AUTHOR

1. WELCOME TO THE BATTLEFIELD

Hey there! Are you ready for an unforgettable journey through one of the most important chapters in history? Buckle up, because we're about to start on an exciting journey through the twists and turns of World War I!

Hold on tight because we're going to explore the pages of history like never before. We'll unearth the mysteries of great battles, meet real-life heroes, and learn about the extraordinary events that changed the world during and after World War 1.

- ***DID YOU KNOW***

But wait - this isn't your typical history lesson. Look out for my facts throughout the book. I've included loads of trivia, incredible war facts, some amazing, some weird, some horrible as well as mind-boggling facts to make learning about this crucial period as exciting as a roller-coaster ride!

Filled with awesome tales of heroism and bravery, you will be transported back into the middle of the First World War. Experience the victories and defeats as if you were on the battlefield with the soldiers!

What Was World War 1?

World War One – the 'Great War' as it was known at the time – was fought between 1914 and 1918.

Wars had been fought for centuries, but never one like this! It was one of the biggest wars in history and involved many countries from around the world.

The war was mostly fought in Europe, but it was called a "World War" because so many different countries were involved in the fighting.

Millions of soldiers and civilians lost their lives during this terrible conflict, and it changed the world forever.

- ***DID YOU KNOW***
    - *Although most of the fighting took place in Europe, **more than 30 countries** were involved in the conflict by the end.*

20 million people lost their lives - more deaths than in any of the battles fought before. **20 million were also wounded!** It would be the first time that a war would be fought on the land, in the air, and on the sea. New inventions like tanks, aircraft, and machine guns meant soldiers and leaders had to adapt quickly or die. The old way of waging war was gone - the modern era was here.

Although the war started because of the killing of an Austrian Archduke, tensions had been building between countries for many years, and the assassination was the final spark to ignite war. Many countries had agreements to support one another if they were threatened by others, and these agreements dragged them all into war.

Soldiers were stationed in trenches, waiting, firing shots at the enemy until one side was brave or reckless enough to charge against the other. Places such as the Somme, Verdun, Ypres, and Meusse-Argonne became known for huge battles where thousands were killed.

The fighting dragged on with victories and defeats for both sides until the United States got involved. Bringing men and artillery with them, they helped to swing the direction of the war against the Germans in 1917. The following year would see the Allies win all the remaining battles and bring an end to the war.

World War 1 changed the world in many ways. After the war, some countries' borders were redrawn, and new countries were created. The war also ended several powerful empires, like the Austro-Hungarian Empire and the Ottoman Empire.

Many people hoped this war would be "**the war to end all wars**," but unfortunately, as we know, it didn't turn out that way. The anger and problems that came from World War 1 eventually helped cause World War 2 just a few decades later.

- *DID YOU KNOW*
  - *The war resulted in the collapse of four major empires:* ***Austro-Hungarian, Ottoman, German, and Russian****.*
  - New countries were created, including **Czechoslovakia Yugoslavia, Finland, Estonia, Latvia and Poland**, as the old empires fell apart, and borders were redrawn.

After reading this book, you will know:

- The causes of the war and who was involved.
- The major battles and the turning points of the war, along with statistics and incredible stories of heroism.
- The new technology and weapons used in the war and the effects they had.
- What it was like to be a soldier in the trenches and what trench warfare was all about.
- What part Winston Churchill played in this war.
- Why President Woodrow Wilson kept America neutral at

first, only joining the war in 1917.

Let's jump into the muddy trenches and find out everything you can about the war that changed the modern world!

2. TIMELINE OF THE WAR

This timeline will help you understand the key events that led to the war, the important battles, and major developments that happened during this time.

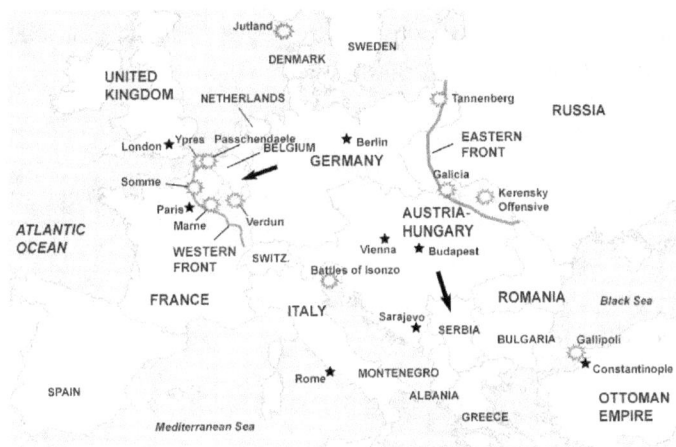

Major WW1 Battlefields

1914

- June 28: Archduke Franz Ferdinand of Austria-Hungary is assassinated in Sarajevo, Bosnia, sparking tensions between countries.

- July 28: One month later, Austria-Hungary declares war on Serbia, starting the war.

- August 1: Germany declares war on Russia, as Russia supports Serbia.

- August 3: Germany declares war on France, following its

plan to attack quickly.

- August 4: Great Britain declares war on Germany after Germany invades Belgium.

- Aug 5: The Battle of Liege.

This was the first battle of the war, considered a moral victory for the Allies, as the heavily outnumbered Belgians held out against the German Army for 12 days, slowing their invasion of France.

- Aug 10: Austria-Hungary invades Russia

- Aug 14: Battle of the Frontiers begins.

The first great clashes on the Western Front. Fought in France and Belgium, the battle results in a series of German victories and Allied retreats.

- Aug 23: Japan declares war on Germany

- Aug 26-30: Battle of Tannenberg

Russia attacks Germany along East Prussia (Poland). At first, the Russians have the upper hand, but ultimately Germany forces Russia to retreat.

- Sept 6-12: 1st Battle of Marne

The French and British manage to stop German forces from entering Paris, just 30 miles from the city. The Germans move their army back to Aisne and the trench war begins.

- Nov 3: Russia declares war on Ottoman Empire

- Nov 5: Britain and France declare war on Ottoman Empire

- Oct–Nov: 1st Battle of Ypres

Trying to win a "race to the sea" and control a strategic port in Belgium, the Germans and Allies get stuck in a trench war that ends with no winner as both sides call it off because of the harsh winter.

- Dec 8: Battle of Falkland Islands

British Navy warships destroy the German squadron of Admiral Graf von Spee in the South Atlantic off the coast of Argentina. Von Spee and two of his sons serving in his squadron are killed.

- Dec 24-25: A Christmas Truce was called

Soldiers who had been fighting in the muddy trenches put down their weapons. Soldiers began to leave their trenches, meeting in the middle to shake hands, exchange small gifts like food, tobacco, and buttons, and even play football!

1915

- Feb 4: Germany blockades Britain with submarines
- Feb–Jan 1916: Battle of Gallipoli, Turkey

The first beach landing saw the Allies try to rush in and take Constantinople from the Turks. What was supposed to be a quick victory turned out to be a long-drawn-out defeat as the Allies were forced to withdraw after losing too many men.

- March 11: Britain blockades German ports
- April–May: 2nd Battle of Ypres

The first German attack with poison gas. After fierce fighting, both sides maintained their lines and advanced no further.

- May 7: German submarine sinks the British ocean liner, the Lusitania

The first passenger liner to be hit, killing many civilians on board.

- May 23: Italy joins the war on the side of the Allies
- June–Nov 1917: Battles of the Isonzo

A series of 12 battles fought between Italy and Austria-Hungary along the Isonzo River. After short, intense attacks, very little gain was made by the Italians, and they were finally pushed back.

- Oct 14: Bulgaria enters the war

1916

- Feb–Dec: Battle of Verdun

The longest battle of WW1, Germany launched a surprise attack against the French that left many dead on both sides. Although the Germans made significant advances at first, they were forced to pull out as the Brusilov Offensive on the Eastern Front, against Russia, meant their troops needed reinforcements.

- Apr 29: Siege of Kut

British forces surrender to Turkish forces at Kut, Mesopotamia (modern day Iraq) after a five-month siege.

- May–June: Battle of Jutland

The only major naval battle of WW1 ends with no real winner.

- June–Aug: Brusilov Offensive

The largest and most successful Allied assault belonged to Russia. Using surprise and numbers, Brusliov (a Russian general) ordered a full-scale attack that almost defeated Austria-Hungary. It also forced the Central Powers to give up the land they had taken from Russia and pull more troops from battles being fought in the West to stop the Russian attack on the Eastern Front.

- July–Nov: 1st Battle of the Somme

One of the bloodiest battles as British troops are cut down trying to run at the German trenches near the Somme River. The British suffer 60,000 casualties in the first day! Although the Allies changed their tactics, there are no real breakthroughs.

1917

- Mar 15: Tsar Nicholas II abdicates

After the Russian Revolution, the Tsar steps down and a provisional government is established. Great Britain, France, the United States, and Italy quickly recognize the new government so Russia might stay in the war on the Eastern Front.

- April 6: America declares war on Germany

After German submarines continued attacking ships and the Zimmerman telegram Germany sent to Mexico encouraging them to attack the US, Woodrow Wilson convinces his country to join the war.

- May 19: Russia stays in the war

The Provisional Government of Russia announces it will stay in the war. A large offensive for the Eastern Front is planned by Alexander Kerensky, the new Minister of War. However, many Russian soldiers and peasants join Lenin's Bolshevik Party which opposes the war and the government.

- May 27–June 1: French soldiers mutiny

French soldiers refuse orders to advance, angry over the battles of attrition and terrible living conditions in the muddy, rat and lice-infested trenches. The new Commander-in-Chief, Henri Petain, cracks down on the mutiny through mass arrests and firing squad executions. With the French Army in disarray, the main burden on the Western Front falls upon the British.

- June 7: Messines Ridge explosion

A huge underground explosion collapses the German-held Messines Ridge south of Ypres.

- June 13: London attacked

London suffers its highest civilian casualties of the war as German airplanes bomb the city, killing 158 people and wounding 425.

- July–Nov: 3rd Battle of Ypres

Known also as the Battle of Passchendaele, a series of attacks and counterattacks in rain and mud ended in the Allies advancing only five miles, at a cost of 500,000 casualties for the Allies and the Central Powers. The Allies claim this as a victory!

- Nov 7: The Russian October Revolution

The Bolsheviks, led by Vladimir Lenin and Leon Trotsky, overthrow the Russian government in the October Revolution. Lenin announces that Soviet Russia will immediately end its involvement in the war and renounces all treaties with the Allies.

- Nov–Dec: Battle of Cambrai

First large-scale tank assault led by the British.

- Dec 9: Britain captures Jerusalem

This ends four centuries of control by the Ottoman Empire.

1918

- Feb 18: Operation Faustschlag

Also known as the Eleven Days War, this is the last major offensive on the Eastern Front. The Central Powers capture huge territories in Estonia, Latvia, Belarus, and Ukraine, forcing the Bolshevik government of Russia to sign the Treaty of Brest-Litovsk, a peace treaty.

- March 3: Russia pulls out of the war

- March–April: 2nd Battle of the Somme

Knowing the Russians are now out of the war, the Germans attack with gas and artillery, pushing the British back. But the assault runs out of steam and the Allies stop the advance.

- March 21: Ludendorff (Spring) Offensive

An attempt to seize the advantage before US troops enter the war, the Germans push hard along the Western Front. Although successful, the land seized is not strategic, and their troops are tired.

- April – 4th Battle of Ypres

Also known as the Battle of the Lys, part of the German spring offensive. Once again, the Germans failed to capture Ypres.

- July 15–18: 2nd Battle of the Marne

In their last main offensive, the Germans attack the Allies but are tricked by false trenches. By the time they reach the real frontline, they are outgunned by French and US troops and forced to retreat.

- Aug 8–11: Battle of Amiens

This battle was part of the Hundred Days Offensive, which was one of the Allies' most successful advances. With a combined artillery, tank, and plane assault, the Germans collapsed.

- Sept–Nov: Battles of the Meuse-Argonne

One million US soldiers take part in battles in the Argonne Forest, and although losing many lives, they force Germany into retreat.

- Sept – 5th Battle of Ypres

This was part of the Hundred Days Offensive. The Allies, including Belgian, British, and French forces, attacked the weakened German army near Ypres and captured much of the territory they'd previously lost. The Allied victory helped to end the war.

- Sept 28: German Kaiser agrees to armistice

Confronted by the strength of the Allies and defeat on the Western Front, Ludendorff and von Hindenburg urge the Kaiser to end the war and ask for an armistice.

- Sept–Nov: Armistices signed by the Central Powers

Austria-Hungary signs an armistice with Italy on November 3rd, leaving Germany alone in the war.

Germany signs the Armistice on November 11th, officially ending World War 1 - victory for the Allies and a defeat for Germany. Fighting continues until 11 a.m., with **2,738 men dying on the last day of the war**.

1919

- June 28: Treaty of Versailles signed

The treaty is signed exactly five years after the death of Archduke Franz Ferdinand. The treaty officially ends the war and places heavy penalties on Germany.

3. WHAT CAUSED WORLD WAR I

The simplest answer would be because an archduke got shot. It seems to be the perfect reason - revenge and retaliation. But the cause of the war is not that simple! There was much more happening behind the scenes where tensions between countries in Europe had been growing for many years.

Mistrust had been brewing after a series of smaller conflicts, and while everyone tried their best to keep the peace and stick to their borders, there were those who were looking for a fight.

Let's take a look at the many factors that lead to war.

1. The Concert of Europe and Rivalries

The Concert of Europe was a system set up after the defeat of Napoleon in 1815. The idea was for the great powers of Europe - Britain, France, Russia, Austria, and later Germany - to work together to keep the peace. For many years, it helped prevent big wars, but over time, it started to break down.

As the 19th century came to an end, countries became more competitive, and old rivalries flared up. Some countries wanted more land, more colonies, or greater influence. This competition led to tensions between major powers, especially as new nations, like Germany and Italy, unified and grew more powerful.

Germany, unified under Otto von Bismarck, in particular, wanted to challenge Britain and France for colonies and influence around the world.

2. Alliances

By the late 1800s and early 1900s, countries in Europe began forming alliances to protect themselves. These alliances were agreements between countries to help each other if one of them was attacked. The two main alliances before World War 1 were:

- **The Triple Entente (Allies)**: This included France, Russia, and Britain.

- **The Triple Alliance (Central Powers)**: This included Germany, Austria-Hungary, and Italy (although Italy later switched sides and joined the Allies during the war).

These alliances were supposed to keep the peace, but they also meant that if one country got into a war, its allies would be dragged in too, making the war much larger.

3. Nationalism

Nationalism is the strong belief that your country is better than others. In the years leading up to World War 1, nationalism was growing across Europe. In some cases, this caused tensions between countries, especially where different nationalities were living under foreign rule. For example:

Serbian nationalism was a big problem for Austria-Hungary. Serbia wanted to unite all the Slavic people in the Balkans, including those living in Austria-Hungary. This made Austria-Hungary nervous because they didn't want to lose control of their Slavic populations.

4. Militarism

Militarism means that countries focus on building up their military forces in readiness for war. In the early 1900s, many European nations were building bigger armies and navies, especially Germany and Britain.

This led to an arms race, with countries competing to have the best weapons and strongest military. With powerful armies ready to go, countries were more likely to solve their problems with war.

5. Imperialism

Imperialism is when countries try to build empires by taking over other lands. European powers, like Britain, France, and Germany, were competing for colonies, especially in Africa and Asia.

This competition for land and resources caused arguments and mistrust between the countries, making the situation in Europe even more tense.

6. Spark – Assassination of Archduke Franz Ferdinand

On June 28th, 1914, Archduke Franz Ferdinand, the heir to the Austro-Hungarian throne, was visiting Sarajevo, a city in Bosnia. Bosnia was part of Austria-Hungary, but many people living there were Serbs who didn't like being ruled by Austria.

A 19-year-old Serbian man called Gavrilo Princip shot and killed the Archduke. Princip thought that killing the Archduke would help end the Austria-Hungarian rule of Bosnia.

- **DID YOU KNOW**
    - *Too young to be given the death penalty, Princip was sen-*

tenced to prison for 20 years, but died of tuberculosis a few months before the end of World War 1.

British soldiers WWI

War Declarations

Austria-Hungary immediately assumed Serbia was behind the assassination and saw the perfect chance to defeat its smaller neighbor once and for all.

Knowing it had the backing of its German allies, Austria-Hungary **declared war a month later on July 28th, 1914,** and began bombing Belgrade, the capital of Serbia, the next day.

Now, here's where the alliances come in and it gets a little complicated! These alliances saw the war spread from its beginnings in the Balkans!

- **Austria-Hungary declared war on Serbia** because of the Archduke's assassination.

- **Germany, Austria-Hungary's ally, promised to help** them if there was a war.

- **Russia was friends with Serbia**, so they promised to help Serbia fight against Austria-Hungary.

- When Russia got involved, **France joined to help Russia** because they had an alliance.

- When **Germany** saw that France and Russia were getting ready to fight, they **declared war on both**.

- When Germany invaded Belgium, **Great Britain declared war on Germany**.

On August 4th, 1914, Germany invaded Belgium on its way to attack France. This was the trigger for Great Britain to step in. It was not concerned with Serbia, the main cause of the whole disagreement in the first place, but it had an agreement to protect Belgium. It was also looking to prevent a French defeat which would have left Germany in control of Western Europe. **On August 4th at 11pm, King George V declared war on Germany**.

Japan declared war on Germany on August 23rd. It saw an opportunity to take control of German territories in Asia and the Pacific, to expand its own influence in the region.

Now we have the 2 sides in the war - Russia, Great Britain, and France secretly signed the Treaty of London, formally binding them together as the Allies versus the Central Powers of Austria-Hungary, Germany, and later Turkey.

Many people accepted the war, thinking it would be over in a few months. But no one had any idea that one assassination would lead to over four years of fighting and death!

Soldiers in gas masks, with machine gun

- **DID YOU KNOW**
  - **World War 1 lasted from July 28th 1914 to November 11th, 1918,** when an armistice was signed (an agreement to stop fighting).
  - Soldiers on the Western Front spent years fighting in trenches, which were often **muddy, filled with rats, and prone to diseases**.
  - **There was a Christmas Truce in 1914.** On Christmas Eve and Christmas Day in 1914, soldiers from both sides

along the Western Front stopped fighting and even sang carols, exchanged gifts, and played football together! The Christmas Truce was special because it showed that even in the middle of a terrible war, soldiers on both sides were still human. They shared a brief moment of peace and kindness, despite being enemies. However, the truce didn't last, and the fighting resumed after the holiday.

- **The longest battle lasted 302 days!** The Battle of Verdun, in northeastern France, was fought between France and Germany, lasted from February to December 1916. The Germans wanted to cause as many casualties as possible and force the French to surrender – in all there were **700,000 killed**, injured or missing from both sides.

- Due to food shortages, **Britons were banned from throwing rice at weddings and feeding pigeons**. They were also banned from talking in a foreign language on the phone and buying binoculars.

4. WHICH COUNTRIES TOOK PART IN THE WAR

What made this different from other wars? Not just the new technology and weapons, but the vast territory it stretched across, from Europe to Africa and the Middle East.

But the main difference was the number of countries that took part - **32 nations declared war** over the course of four years. Many of these were European, but others like Japan and the United States changed it from being a continental squabble into a full-blown world war.

Some chose not to get involved, and remained neutral. Others were forced to join because they had promised to help another country that was being picked on.

There were others, like the United States, which were dragged in reluctantly when they became the targets of Germany's submarine warfare.

- ***DID YOU KNOW***
    - Some of the other countries that declared war:
    - **Romania** *(joined the Allies in 1916)*
    - **Greece** *(joined the Allies in 1917)*
    - **Portugal** *(declared war on Germany in 1916)*
    - **Brazil** *(the only South American country to declare war, siding with the Allies in 1917)*

As in any war, there were two main sides: the Central Powers, who started the conflict by declaring war, and the Allies, who responded to their aggressive military actions. The Allies had more countries on their side and a larger number of soldiers, which gave them a significant advantage over their enemies.

In total, **60 million soldiers responded to the call to fight** for their side, making it the largest manned war in history up to that date.

Central Powers

This group is seen as being the aggressors, as they were the first to declare war for their own selfish goals.

The countries in this alliance were eager to expand their empires by force or manipulation, expecting only brief, limited conflicts instead of a long, global war.

Let's see who made up the Central Powers.

1. Germany

Although Austria-Hungary was the largest in terms of size and people, it was Germany that took the lead in the war as it had the biggest army and the most weapons. After unifying all the smaller kingdoms within its region into one proud nation, it set about mobilizing a massive armed force which included amassing one of the largest navies at the time.

Germany wasn't just trying to expand its borders; it was also worried about being surrounded - Germany was caught between two countries it didn't trust: France and Russia.

Germany's plan was to protect itself by defeating France quickly and then turning to fight Russia. But things didn't go as they expected. Instead of just one quick battle, Germany's actions started a big war on two sides at the same time, making things much harder for them.

The Western and Eastern Fronts became the main areas where troops clashed. On the west, Germany fought France and Britain, while the east saw them tackle Russia. Fighting on two fronts put a huge strain on the German army.

- **DID YOU KNOW**

    - *Out of a population of 65 million, Germany suffered **1.7 million military deaths** and 430,000 civilian deaths.*

    - *With the Allied blockage of German ports, there was not enough food to feed everyone. After a very cold winter in 1916-17, some **people suffered from malnutrition and some even starved***

2. Austria-Hungary

Austria-Hungary felt it had to prove itself. With its old emperor, Franz Joseph, getting close to the end of his rule, it wanted to show that it was still a strong power and not becoming weak.

Austria-Hungary wanted to crush Serbia, protect its borders, and show its power, so it declared war. But Austria-Hungary wouldn't have done this without the support of its close friend, Germany. Their promise to help each other gave Austria-Hungary the confidence to go ahead with its plan.

3. The Ottoman Empire

The Ottoman Empire, once one of the world's most powerful kingdoms, was starting to lose its strength. The Balkan countries were rebelling, which hurt the empire's pride and shrank its borders. At the start of the war, the Ottoman Empire stayed out of it and was seen as an outsider. It talked with both sides - the Central Powers and the Allies - before secretly making a deal with Germany on July 30th, 1914, hoping to gain land from Russia.

Instead of declaring war right away, the Ottomans tried to get Russia to attack first so they could join the fight and claim it was in self-defense.

4. Bulgaria

Bulgaria tried to remain neutral. But both the Central Powers and Allies tried to convince the country to join its side, and after seeing a chance for revenge for losing the Balkan Wars, it jumped in with the Central Powers.

- *DID YOU KNOW*
  - *By 1918, 900,000 Bulgarian men, nearly 40% of the male population, had been conscripted (forced to join the army). The army suffered 300,000 casualties, including **100,000 killed, the most losses per head** of any country involved in the war.*

Allied Powers

At first, the Allies were a group of countries called the Triple Entente, which was formed before the war started. These nations were fighting back because they believed Germany and Austria-Hungary were attacking other countries' independence.

Unlike their enemies, the Allies were not interested in claiming more territory – instead they wanted to protect their neighbors from these attacks. As the war went on, more countries joined the Allies, creating a large Allied and Affiliated Force.

Let's see who made up the Allies:

1. Great Britain

Great Britain was primarily focused on maintaining the balance of power in Europe. It saw Germany's growing military and aggressive actions as a threat to that balance, which could destabilize the whole of Europe.

Since it had one of the biggest navies at that time, Britain saw its role as one of preventing German expansion. It was also committed to protecting Belgium, and once German forces invaded Belgium, there was no other choice but to declare war.

- *DID YOU KNOW*
    - ***880,000 British soldiers died in the war***, *and 70,000 civilians. So many men died that the census of 1921 showed 109 women for every 100 men.*
    - *British soldiers were nicknamed '**Tommies**' by German soldiers, while the British called the Germans '**Jerry**' or '**Fritz**'.*

2. France

France viewed Great Britain as a friendly nation but had a much stronger alliance with Russia at the time. This pact was seen as a threat by Germany. France supported its ally, Russia, setting it firmly against the Central Powers.

With **3.5 million soldiers**, France was hopeful of a quick victory in the war. However, as the fighting dragged on, it had to reevaluate its war strategy.

- **DID YOU KNOW**
  - ○ ***1.4 million French soldiers died***, *with half dying between the start of the war and 1915.*
  - ○ ***4.2 million*** *(71% of those fighting) were wounded.*

3. Russia

Russia was the largest country involved in the war, with the most people and resources. However, it remained primarily an agricultural economy, with its manufacturing ability and factory output lagging far behind those of other countries. This led to a weak military presence and ineffective leadership under Tsar Nicholas II. Unlike its allies, Russia wanted to gain more land through fighting. It strongly supported Serbia, setting it against Austria-Hungary when the war started.

When the Ottoman Empire joined the war, Russia saw a chance to take land along the Mediterranean Sea to become more powerful in that area.

- **DID YOU KNOW**
  - ○ *Estimates of the numbers of Russian soldiers killed range from **1.8 million to 2.2 million!***

British prisoners of war

Others Involved

At the signing of the peace treaty at the end of the war, there were 27 countries listed alongside the Allies. Many only joined towards the end once the US entered the fighting.

Japan's involvement in the war was more about taking advantage of the situation than fighting. There was no fighting in Japan itself, and it only had about 2,000 soldiers hurt during the entire conflict. Instead, Japan used its strong navy and resources to help stop the Germans from taking control of the oceans. Since Japan had an alliance with Great Britain, it was quick to offer help.

- *DID YOU KNOW*
  - *The Japanese defeat of German forces at Tsingtao in 1914, was the first time seaplanes were used to sink a German warship.*

At first, Italy was on the side of Austria-Hungary and Germany, but when the war started, it decided to stay neutral and not fight. Later on, Italy chose to join the Allies, with 5 million men in its army by 1918!

Belgium, Greece, Montenegro, Romania, and Serbia all supported the Allies, with a combined force of 1.5 million soldiers and was heavily involved in many of the battles.

The USA joined the war later than most countries. President Woodrow Wilson was hesitant to enter, but he believed it was important for Americans to support the war by providing supplies and money. Although American soldiers didn't arrive until 1917, their timing was perfect because Russia had to leave the war due to problems at home.

With 4.3 million soldiers ready to fight, the American soldiers had not yet spent time in the muddy trenches that many soldiers faced in the first half of World War 1, making them fresh and excited to get involved. The USA's involvement helped turn the tide of the war in favor of the Allies.

- **DID YOU KNOW**

    - *__320,000 American soldiers were killed__, and 204,000 wounded.*

    - *Woodrow Wilson used the slogan "__He kept us out of war__" when he ran for his second term as president. But after he was sworn in, about a month later, he changed his mind and declared war on Germany.*

    - *Even though __Native Americans__ weren't officially given U.S. citizenship until 1924, nearly __13,000 of them bravely fought__ in World War I.*

There were many other countries that fought out of loyalty, especially those belonging to the British Empire, such as Canada, Australia, New Zealand, South Africa, and India, who all signed up to fight under the British crown.

5. WORLD WAR I IN NUMBERS

This war was like nothing anyone had ever seen before. There were more soldiers and weapons than ever, and countries used everything they had in battles that lasted for days, months, and even years.

It was not just bigger but also included new things like planes, tanks, and submarines, which had never been used in wars before.

The money spent was enormous, but the loss of lives was the most heartbreaking part of it all.

Shocking Numbers

- **32** - Nations which officially declared war
- **65 million** - Soldiers that took part in the war
- **9.7 million** - Deaths of soldiers in battle
- **10 million** - Deaths of civilians
- **8 million** - Horses killed in action
- **6 million** - Prisoners of war
- **1.5 billion** - Explosive shells fired on the Western Front
- **220,000** - Aircraft produced for the war
- **7,700** - Tanks produced for the war (Germany only made 20!)
- **5,000** - Ships lost at sea from U-boat (submarine) attacks

- **$186 billion ($334 billion equivalent today)** - Total cost of the war

Surprising Numbers

- **12** – The age of Sydney Lewis when he joined the army – the youngest soldier in the war. He was too young to join the army, but had lied about his age!

- **67** – The age of Thomas Enright, the oldest known soldier in WWI.

- **2 billion** - Letters delivered to the soldiers on the frontline

- **35,000 miles** - The entire length of trenches dug during the war

- **140 miles** - An explosion in Belgium could be heard that far away in London

- **11/11/11** - The Armistice was signed at 11 am on 11th November 1918

- **500,000** - Pigeons used to carry messages between headquarters and the frontlines

- **5ft 3ins** - The minimum height required to serve in the British Army, but "bantam battalions" were created for those who were shorter!

- **1 minute** - Henry Gunther was killed 60 seconds before the Armistice was announced, making him the last soldier killed in action

- **90%** - The percentage of the 7.8 million soldiers from Austria-Hungary who fought in the war that were either injured or killed

- **14** - The age of Private John Condon, who was the youngest Allied soldier killed, who died in a gas attack during the Second Battle of Ypres in 1915

- **16,000** — The number of British conscientious objectors who refused to fight in the war. Men refused because of religious or moral reasons. They faced mistreatment and prison. Many were handed a white feather as a sign of cowardice and to try to shame them into fighting.

Deadly Figures

The number of soldiers hurt or killed in a war helps us understand how big each battle was. Instead of making the war seem exciting, these numbers should remind us of how many lives were lost.

In World War 1, many men died because of poor decisions or not knowing how to fight in new, modern ways.

1. Hundred Days Offensive – August 1918

1,855,369 casualties (killed, captured or missing) - Germans 785,733, Allies 1,069,636 (incl. 127,000 Americans)

The Germans were defeated which led to the end of the war.

2. The Spring Offensive – March 1918

1,539,715 casualties - Germans 680,000, Allies 850,000

The Allies halted the advance of the German troops.

3. Battle of the Somme – July 1916

1,219,201 casualties - Germans 800,000, Allies 623,906

The Somme is an example of the senseless slaughter of the war.

19,240 British soldiers were killed on the 1st day!

4. Battle of Verdun – February 1916

976,000 casualties - Germans 435,000, French 542,000

Over 40 million artillery shells fired during the battle.

5. The Battle of Passchendaele

848,614 casualties - Germans 400,000, Allies 448,614

Part of the Third Battle of Ypres, in Flanders, Belgium. The conditions were terrible, and both sides lost many soldiers. Even though the British fought hard, they only gained a small amount of land.

6. The Serbian Campaign – July 1914

633,500 casualties

A series of battles between Austria-Hungary and Serbia. During the whole war, Serbian losses equalled 27% of its total population and 60% of its male population.

7. The First Battle of the Marnes – September 1914

483,000 casualties - Germans 220,000, Allies 263,000

The battle that ended the German invasion of France and led to trench warfare.

8. The Gallipoli Campaign – February 1915

473,000 casualties - Turks 253,000, Allies 220,000

The Allies wanted to break the stalemate on the Western Front and help the Russians by creating a sea route to the east, near Turkey, to send supplies. However, their plan didn't work, and it ended in a disaster.

9. Battle of Arras – April 1917

278,000 casualties - Germans 120,000, Allies 158,000

For two years, the Western Front didn't move much, with both sides losing millions of soldiers in battles like Verdun and the Somme. The Allies decided to attack the trenches near the town of Arras. While the British won the battle, it wasn't the big success they had hoped for.

10. Battle of Tannenberg – August 1914

182,000 total casualties - Russians 170,000, Germans 12,000

The Germans won an important battle, even though they had fewer soldiers than two Russian armies. They defeated almost the entire second army and most of the first army, making it a big victory for them.

6. TACTICS AND TECHNOLOGY

World War 1 completely changed how battles were fought. The old way of fighting face-to-face on the frontlines was gone. New technology meant armies had to find new ways to defend and attack. Sometimes, soldiers could be in danger without even knowing the enemy was watching them!

But the leaders of the armies were slow to understand how best to fight with these new weapons, and it cost many lives. The soldiers, brave and strong, followed orders even when the plans were outdated, and people often said they were "lions being led by donkeys" – suggesting the soldiers were strong and capable, but their commanders were not good at leading them, resultIng in many unnecessary deaths.

- **DID YOU KNOW**
  - *One myth is that the generals stayed far away from danger while the ordinary soldiers fought in the muddy trenches. While some senior officers didn't see much fighting, this wasn't true for all of them. In fact, during the war, **78 British generals were killed**.*

Small Armies to Mass Conscription

Let's see how armies changed to meet the demands of this new form of warfare, by looking at how the British Army changed.

Before the war, the British Army was mostly small and used to stop revolts or uprisings in parts of its Empire. But during World War 1, it grew much bigger as many civilians - regular people who didn't know much about war - joined to help. Officers weren't used to managing such a large and inexperienced group, and it took a lot of time to figure out how to handle this massive army.

By late 1917, after learning some hard lessons, the soldiers and generals started fighting more effectively and with better strategies.

- **Before the War**: The British Army was a small, professional force. It was made up mostly of career soldiers, known for their discipline and training.

- **After the War Began**: As the war dragged on and casualties mounted, Britain needed more soldiers. This led to the **introduction of conscription** in 1916, where men were required to join the army. The army grew from around **80,000 professional soldiers** at the start of the war to an army of over **5 million men** by the end.

- **The Decline of the "Old Redoubtables".** The Old Redoubtables refers to the seasoned, professional soldiers from the pre-war British Army. Many of these men were part of the **British Expeditionary Force** (BEF) that fought in the early stages of the war, especially in battles like **Mons** and **Le Cateau**.

- Sadly, many of these soldiers were killed or wounded in the early years of the war, especially in 1914 and 1915. They were known for their experience and skill, but as the war went on, they were replaced by a much larger, less experienced army made up of volunteers and conscripts.

- **The Pals Battalions.** In the early years of the war, many men volunteered to fight alongside their friends and coworkers. These groups were known as **Pals Battalions**. However, the heavy losses they suffered, especially in battles like the **Somme**, had a devastating impact on communities back home, as entire groups of men from the same town or neighborhood were killed or wounded.

British soldiers WWI

Changing How Wars Are Fought

Before World War 1, the British Army fought in various conflicts, and its methods of warfare were shaped by historical practices and the technologies available at the time. Let's look at how it fought wars and battles before 1914.

1. Types of Warfare

- **Colonial Warfare**: Before World War 1, the British Army spent a lot of time fighting in different parts of the world to keep control of their empire. They would stop rebellions, protect British land, or try to gain more territory, often fighting against weak or disorganised opposition. These fights happened in places like Africa, India, and other regions in Asia and the Americas.

- **Traditional Battles:** The British Army also fought in more traditional battles against other European countries. In these battles, soldiers would line up and fire their weapons in groups, believing that this was the best way to win.

- **Limited Mobility**: Battles didn't involve much movement. Armies would try to capture important positions and directly attack their enemies. There wasn't as much focus on moving quickly as there would be in later wars.

2. Tactics and Organization

- **Lining Up to Fight:** Soldiers used to stand in long lines to make the most of their muskets or rifles. They would fire all together in groups, called volleys, and had to be very disciplined and follow orders carefully to keep things organized.

- **Cavalry:** Cavalry units, made up of soldiers on horses, were very important. They were used to explore the battlefield, attack from the sides, or chase after the enemy if they were running away.

- **Big Cannons (Artillery):** Artillery was very important in battles. The British Army used cannons and other big guns to attack enemy positions before sending in soldiers. As technology improved, these cannons became much more powerful and accurate, changing how wars were fought.

As we can see, in the past, wars were often won by wearing the enemy down over time. Armies would keep attacking, hoping that the other side would get too tired to fight back. They would fire big cannons for a long time and then slowly send their soldiers to advance. This way of fighting took a long time and caused a lot of soldiers to lose their lives. Many of the generals in World War 1 had learned to fight this way in earlier wars, so they thought it would work again.

WWI artillery

However, against trenches and new technology, the old ways of fighting didn't work and cost many lives! World War 1 has often been called a "pointless bloodbath" because of how many people died without much progress. But the war also made people change how they thought about fighting. Generals had to learn new strategies, though some were slower to understand than others.

Horses had been really useful in battles before, but they couldn't get through the muddy trenches and barbed wire on the Western Front, so they weren't good for attacks. Even though there were armored vehicles, they were too slow, hard to drive, and often got stuck in the mud. When soldiers managed to break through enemy lines, it took too long for the rest of the army to catch up, and surprise attacks would often fail. Both sides ended up stuck in their trenches, with no-one winning, while leaders tried to figure out better ways to win the war.

World War 1 made leaders rethink how wars should be fought, and by the end of the war, there were three big changes in the way battles were planned for the future.

1. Machines not men

Battles were no longer about the strength of soldiers and horses; now, machines were in charge. The cavalry wasn't leading the frontlines anymore, and soldiers couldn't run faster than bullets! Engines, tanks, trucks, and other vehicles started to take over the battlefield.

A good example of this change in thinking is General Haig. At first, he led the unsuccessful battles of Passchendaele and the Somme, where he kept sending his men into long, tough fights without changing his tactics. But later, he realized that tanks could be very effective if used the right way and helped improve them for future battles.

2. Three-dimensional war

War used to be fought on land and at sea, but everything changed with the invention of airplanes. Suddenly, soldiers had to watch out for attacks coming from above as well as in front and behind them. Generals now had to think about controlling the skies, which was a brand-new idea!

The battle at Amiens in 1918 shows how the Allies changed their strategy from two years earlier during the Somme. They used quick, strong attacks with both planes and ground troops to surprise the Germans.

Also, the oceans became more complicated with the introduction of submarines in World War 1. Instead of just looking out at the horizon, admirals and captains had to be careful about what was lurking beneath the water, too. Battleships, which had been the kings of the seas for so long, were now vulnerable from both above and below!

3. Deeper frontlines

In the past, the soldiers standing right in front of the enemy were the most at risk. But when airplanes joined the war, it became clear that everyone was in danger, no matter where they were on the battlefield. The soldiers in the middle and back of the army were just as exposed, so the strategies needed to change to handle these new threats.

Before 1914, it was like playing a regular game of chess. But then it suddenly turned into a game where you had to move ten pieces at once to keep up! War had become much more complicated!

Uniforms and Soldiers

It seems funny to think that some officers still wore **swords and rode horses** into battle when there were machine guns and tanks fighting alongside and against them!

Surprisingly, many soldiers wore **cloth caps and had bayonets** on the ends of their rifles, believing that fighting up close was still the best way to go.

Many of these old ideas had to change to keep up with the fast and fierce way wars were being fought. The British had learned this lesson the hard way during the Boer Wars in South Africa when they marched across the battlefield in **bright red uniforms**, making them easy targets for the enemy. This time, **they wore khaki**, the color that the Boers had used so well against them. The Germans chose a neutral grey, which worked really well, too.

However, the French were much slower to change from their old Napoleonic uniforms. They started the war **wearing blue tunics and red trousers**, with their officers even **wearing white gloves**! Can you imagine how easy it would be for the enemy to spot these poor soldiers!

They soon realized they needed to blend in better on the battlefield, so they changed their uniforms and adopted the khaki color.

Along with these changes, in 1908, the British started using webbed pouches and ammunition belts to help carry their heavy supplies and move around more easily in the field. Even with these improvements, the equipment they had to carry still weighed over 70 pounds (32kg)!

Typically a soldier carried a full pack, 250 rounds of ammunition, water bottle, mess kit for eating meals, gas masks, entrenching tool (a small shovel for digging trenches) haversack (a small backpack), rifle, bayonet and any personal items.

Many changes were made to help soldiers move quickly and fight smarter. For example, their normal tall boots were replaced with shorter ones that had cloth wraps around them to keep dirt and stones out.

None of the soldiers wore metal helmets in 1914. The French were the first to introduce them in 1915. Future prime minister Winston Churchill wore a French one during his time on the front in 1916.

Helmet saves head from shrapnel!

New Technologies

Tanks

This new invention had mixed results in the war. Tanks, which were first called "landships" and later named "tanks" because they looked like big water tanks, were more of a problem than a help at first. The early tanks were hard to drive, needed big crews to run them, and didn't work as well as people had hoped.

British WW1 tank

The British first used tanks at the Battle of the Somme in 1916. They worked for a short time but didn't have much effect on the battle. In fact, they accidentally caused more harm to their own soldiers more than the enemy.

The French tried using them later, but the tanks got stuck in rough terrain. Because of this, German General Ludendorff didn't think tanks were very useful, except for breaking through defenses. The Germans built only 20 tanks, while the Allies made 7,000! Instead, the Germans focused on creating ways to stop tanks, which worked really well in battles.

It wasn't until WW2 that tanks became faster, more powerful, and played a huge role in battles.

- **DID YOU KNOW**
  - *British tanks were given **genders**" during the war. **The male tanks had cannons, and the female tanks had machine guns**. The very first tank ever built was called **Little Willie!***

Machine Guns

One of the most important inventions that changed war was the rapid-firing gun. In the past, soldiers had to reload their rifles after every shot, but in 1883, Hiram Maxim invented the first automatic gun. By 1914, many companies were making guns that could fire lots of bullets quickly. This made it very hard for soldiers to charge at the enemy without being stopped by a shower of bullets, which is why WW1 turned into a trench war, with both sides digging in to avoid being hit.

Different strategies were tried, like grouping machine guns together at the Battle of Loos on September 26th, 1915, and at the Somme on July 1st, 1916, to focus their firepower on the enemy with deadly results.

But when newer, lighter machine guns like the Lewis Gun were introduced, soldiers could move around more easily. Small groups of troops, armed with machine guns and grenades, started to figure out a more flexible way to attack, making them faster and more effective in battle.

- **DID YOU KNOW**
  - Machine guns could fire up to **600 rounds per minute**.

- Machine guns **needed to be kept cool with water or even urine** – yuk!

Flamethrowers

The Germans were the first to use flamethrowers in WW1. Led by an officer named Bernhard Reddemann, the Germans used flamethrowers for the first time at Malancourt on February 26th, 1915, to surprise and scare their enemies.

They were especially successful at the Battle of Verdun, and Reddemann was given his own unit of soldiers trained just to use flamethrowers.

Other countries also tried using them, but none used flamethrowers as often or as effectively as the Germans did.

Flamethrowers were very dangerous because they could force soldiers out of their trenches without damaging the trenches themselves. The idea of being burned was really scary for the soldiers, and generals had to come up with ways to protect their troops from this new weapon or find ways to use it themselves. It's pretty awful to think that this kind of thing was used in war!

- **DID YOU KNOW**
  - Flamethrowers could fire a jet of flame **20 yards (18 meters)**.
  - There were two types of flamethrowers: **backpack** and **tank-mounted**. The backpack type was light enough for a soldier to carry, while the tank-mounted type had a longer range.

Air Support

Taking to the air was a new way of fighting, and balloons and Zeppelins (airships) became common sights over battlefields during the war. Mainly used to spy on enemy formations or to drop bombs on strategic locations, the skies became a new frontline. But it was the plane that completely changed the way battles were fought.

Only 15 years after the Wright brothers made their first successful flight, aircraft were introduced into war for the first time.

Sopwith Camel airplane

Many of the early planes were pretty simple. At first, they were mostly used for watching the enemy and sending back information. But once they were equipped with weapons, planes became dangerous fighters.

In 1917, the Germans introduced the Junkers J-1, which had three machine guns and could carry bombs. Even though the Allies had twice as many planes, the Germans were very good at using their ground artillery to take them down!

- ***DID YOU KNOW***
  - *The most successful fighter pilot was the **Red Baron**.*

> Manfred Albrecht Freiherr von Richthofen was a German pilot who **shot down 80 planes**. He died after his plane was brought down near Amiens in 1918
>
> - The term *"**dogfight**"* was used to describe planes fighting each other. The name came from pilots turning the engine off so it would not stall when they turned the planes quickly in the air. When the engine restarted in mid-air, it sounded like dogs barking.

Poison Gas

Gas masks became an important part of the soldiers' gear during the war because countries were trying out chemical weapons. Even though a big meeting called the Hague Peace Conference in 1899 wanted to stop the use of gas attacks, both sides ended up using them.

The fear of gas was often more frightening than the number of soldiers it actually harmed. While it wasn't always effective - since it needed perfect weather and the wind blowing in the right direction – it still gave one side a mental advantage.

- **DID YOU KNOW**
  - Early in the war, the only protection against gas attacks was a **cloth soaked in a soldier's own urine**!

The French used tear gas, and the Germans surprised the Allies with chlorine gas at Ypres on April 22nd, 1915. Phosgene was responsible for more deaths than other gases, but mustard gas was the scariest because it lingered in the air for a long time, causing painful blisters on anyone who got close, even days later.

In total, around 30 different types of gas were used, resulting in about 91,000 deaths. Eventually, all the countries agreed to stop using chemical weapons and signed treaties to ban them.

Tracer Bullets

The invention of tracer bullets changed how soldiers fought at night. Before, they would shoot in the dark and hope to hit something. But with tracer bullets, soldiers could see where their shots were going!

These special bullets had a flammable material at the back, which made them light up as they flew through the air. This helped soldiers adjust their aim and became a great way to target the German Zeppelins that were dropping bombs on England during the night.

- ***DID YOU KNOW***
  - *Women worked in ammunition factories while the men were fighting. Those who handled shells filled with TNT (an explosive compound) were called **"Canary Girls"** because their **skin and hair turned yellow** from exposure to the chemical.*

Wireless Communication

Let's look at how soldiers communicated changed during World War I. They still used runners, dogs, and pigeons to send messages between their bases and the front lines. But at the same time, troops were trying to use new inventions like wireless telegraphy to communicate quicker.

Britain relied on telephones, while the Germans were building wireless towers. When the Allied telephone cables were destroyed during the Battle of the Somme in 1916, the British realized how useful wireless communication was and started putting more effort into this new technology.

Signals office

At the start of the war, soldiers used Morse code to send messages, but by the end, radios became much more popular and changed the way they communicated on the battlefield.

With many countries sharing important plans through radio waves, armies realized they needed people who could understand this technology to listen in on messages. For example, the Germans were able to learn important information about Russian tactics during the Battle of Tannenberg in 1914 because they intercepted radio messages.

- *DID YOU KNOW*
  - *The job of runners during the war was so dangerous that sometimes **three runners were sent with the same***

message *to make sure at least one of them could cross open ground under enemy fire and deliver it. Private James Miller was a brave runner during the Battle of the Somme. On July 30th, 1916, he was shot in the back as he left the trench to deliver a message. Even though he was badly hurt, he held his wound closed, delivered the message, and brought back the answer before collapsing and passing away.*

Mobile X-Ray Machines

Marie Curie is famous for discovering radium and polonium, which are important for understanding radioactivity. But she also invented the first portable x-ray machines! This invention allowed doctors to see what was wrong with injured soldiers close to the front lines, instead of having to transport them far away to the nearest hospital.

To make these x-ray machines work, Curie put a special device called a dynamo in each car, and they became known as "Little Curies." They were first used during the Battle of Marne in 1914.

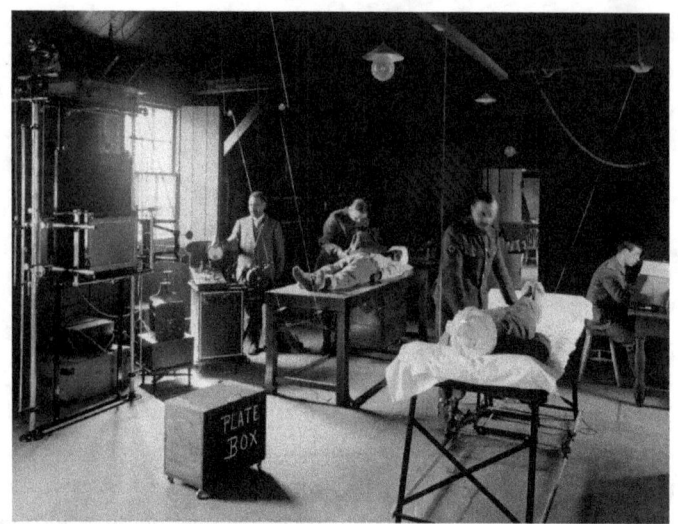

X-ray room at Kitchener Hospital

- **DID YOU KNOW**

  ○ Even with all the new technology during the war, an **elephant named Lizzie was used to help**! In 1914, Lizzie was brought in to carry heavy loads of scrap metal, machinery, and munitions around the city of Sheffield to support the war effort.

7. LEADERS AND GENERALS

In every war, there are brave soldiers waiting to fight, charging at the enemy, or sadly losing their lives on the front lines. But they are often seen as just "boots on the ground." Even though they fight hard, the outcome of the war is usually decided by just a few people making important choices.

Victory or defeat often depends on the generals, who plan everything carefully on maps and organize their troops, cannons, and ships—they are like the brains behind the battle.

But even the generals don't always control the whole war. Far away from the mud and noise of fighting, there are politicians using their power to influence events for their own purposes.

Let's take a look at the men with the power to change the direction and the result of a war.

Allied Political Leaders and Military Generals

Great Britain

- **Herbert Asquith – Prime Minster to 1916**

Asquith was Prime Minister when World War I started in 1914. To maximise government support he formed a coalition in 1915, but this government was unsuccessful and unpopular as the war was going badly.

Some people thought Asquith wasn't making fast enough decisions or leading the war efforts well. Many in the government and the military wanted changes, like stronger leadership to win the war.

In 1916, Asquith decided to step down as Prime Minister because of these pressures. He was replaced by David Lloyd George, who promised to make quicker decisions and focus more on winning the war.

David Lloyd George – Prime Minister from 1916

From 1914 to 1915, Lloyd George was the minister of munitions, which meant he was in charge of bombs, bullets, and explosives. Despite fierce resistance, he pushed through a bold move to increase the production of these items. In 1916, when the Battle of the Somme began, there was no shortage of supplies because of Lloyd George's efforts.

When he became Prime Minister in 1916 one of his biggest jobs was solving the problem of German submarines, which were causing food shortages in Britain. He made sure that warships traveled with merchant ships in a convoy system to protect them. He also encouraged more farming so that Britain would have enough food.

However, his efforts in the war were sometimes not as effective, and he often disagreed with Generals Haig and Kitchener. At the end of the war, Lloyd George's skills in negotiation helped make the Treaty of Versailles less harsh than it could have been.

- **Lord Horatio Kitchener – Secretary of State for War**

Kitchener was a brave and respected officer who received a special title, Baron of Khartoum, for his work in Sudan. He later led the army during the Second Boer War in South Africa, where he used a method called the "scorched earth policy." This approach helped the army but was also controversial because it meant destroying land and resources.

Kitchener's Recruitment Poster

Many people expected the war to be over by Christmas 1914, but Kitchener was one of the few who realized it would be a long war on a huge scale, and encouraged others to prepare for this.

He helped change the British army into a more modern force and launched a recruitment campaign. One of the most famous posters from this campaign showed Lord Kitchener pointing directly at the viewer with the words, **"Your Country Needs YOU."**

Sadly, on June 5th, 1916, while he was traveling on the HMS Hampshire to meet Tsar Nicholas II to talk about battle plans, the ship hit a German mine, and he lost his life along with 736 others.

- **Field Marshall Sir Douglas Haig – Commander in Chief of the British Army**

Haig was put in charge of the British Expeditionary Force (BEF), which was the largest group of soldiers the UK had ever sent into battle. He believed in a strategy called war of attrition, which meant that the longer the fighting went on, the more enemies would be defeated, even if many soldiers lost their lives.

During the battles of the Somme in 1916 and Passchendaele in 1917, his plans led to a huge number of casualties, as he continued to push for victory even when it seemed impossible.

However, by 1918, Haig started using a new approach called the "All Arms" strategy. This involved combining tanks, artillery, infantry, cavalry, and air power in attacks. This new method worked very well during the Hundred Days War, leading to great successes on the battlefield.

Haig was great at using words to inspire his soldiers. One of his most famous messages was called the "Backs to the Wall" communiqué. In this message, he encouraged the men by saying:

"Many amongst us now are tired. To those I would say that victory will belong to the side which holds out the longest. The French Army is moving rapidly and in great force to our support. There is no other course open to us but to fight it out. Every position must be held to the last man: there must be no retirement. With our backs to the wall and believing in the justice of our cause each one of us must fight on to the end."

Despite the criticism Haig received for the high number of casualties in these battles, he led the British forces to victory in 1918. Haig's strategies helped wear down the German army, contributing to the eventual Allied victory.

After the war, Haig worked to support ex-soldiers, helping to create the Royal British Legion to aid veterans.

- ***DID YOU KNOW***
  - *The BEF was the most well-trained European force with the average soldier being able to **hit a target 300 yards away 15 times in a minute** with a Lee-Enfield Rifle.*

Winston Churchill – First Lord of the Admiralty

During World War I, Winston Churchill played a significant role in the British government. At the beginning of the war, he was the First Lord of the Admiralty, in charge of the navy. He wanted to find new ways to break the deadlock on the Western Front in France, where fighting had become very difficult and slow.

One of his most famous ideas was the Dardanelles expedition. Churchill thought that if the British navy could take control of the Dardanelles Strait, in Turkey, they could help the Russians, and open up a new front against the enemy. However, the naval attack did not go well, and many ships and men were lost. Because of this failure, he resigned from his government position.

But Churchill didn't give up. He went to the front lines to serve as an officer and experience what the soldiers were going through. Later, he returned to politics and was appointed as the minister of munitions, where he helped make sure the soldiers had the weapons and supplies they needed to fight.

Churchill's experiences during the war would later shape his leadership during World War II.

- **DID YOU KNOW**
  - In 1917, the King changed the Royal Family's name from the Germanic Saxe-Coburg-Gotha to Windsor.

Russia

Tsar Nicholas II – Emperor of Russia

Nicholas II (pictured left with his cousin George V) was the last emperor of Russia. At first, many people in Russia supported the war because they wanted to defend their country.

Unfortunately, the Russian army was not well-prepared for the war. They lacked enough weapons, food, and supplies. Many Russian soldiers died, and there were many defeats on the battlefield. The tsar decided to take personal command of the army in 1915, even though he had little experience, but the war continued to go badly for Russia.

The war did not go well for Russia. The Russian army suffered many defeats, and soldiers didn't have enough supplies like food, clothing, and weapons. This made people angry at Tsar Nicholas, blaming him for the losses.

At the same time, things were getting worse at home. Food shortages and poverty made life very hard for Russian families, and many people started protesting against the government.

On July 16th, 1918, Tsar Nicholas was removed from power and executed by a group called the Bolsheviks. This marked the end of the Romanov family's rule in Russia.

- **Aleksey Brusilov**

The leader of the South-West Front of the Imperial Russian Army, General Brusilov, became famous for a surprise attack known as the Brusilov Offensive. After facing several defeats, he came up with a new tactic.

Instead of attacking one main point like many other generals, he planned attacks along a wide front (many areas at once) to confuse the enemy. He didn't let the Austro-Hungarian forces know exactly where the main attack would come from. This confused the enemy and forced them to defend many places at once, stretching their forces thin.

Instead of relying on large waves of soldiers charging across open fields (which was common in trench warfare), Brusilov used small, specialized units of soldiers. These units were well-trained and moved quickly, attacking weak spots in the enemy's defenses.

Brusilov's tactics were incredibly successful at first. The Austro-Hungarian army suffered massive losses, and Brusilov was able to advance 20 miles and capture 400,000 enemy soldiers!

This was one of the most successful attacks of the war and showed everyone how to effectively attack trenches.

France

- **Georges Clemenceau – Prime Minister**

As the leader of France during the war, Clemenceau called for men to join the army and made sure they had enough guns and ammunition. He sent many messages to the U.S. President, Woodrow Wilson, asking for America to help in the fight.

Clemenceau believed in winning no matter what and had no patience for traitors or cowards. He's famous for saying, "We'll fight until the last minute, and that last minute will be ours!"

When the war ended, Clemenceau wanted Germany to pay for its role in starting the war. He played a big part in deciding the rules of the Treaty of Versailles.

- **General Joseph Joffre – Commander of French Army**

Known as the "Silent General," Joffre was in charge of the French forces on the Western Front during the war. He became famous for helping the French army when they were retreating, turning things around, and leading them to a big victory in the First Battle of the Marne.

- **Ferdinand Foch – Supreme Allied Commander on Western Front, 1918**

Foch was an important French leader during WW1. He always stayed positive, but sometimes his optimism meant he didn't know when to stop attacking, which caused problems for his soldiers. He led a big victory at the First Battle of the Marne, but after some bad decisions, he was replaced.

Later in the war, Foch was brought back to lead the Allied Forces. He helped stop the Germans during their Ludendorff Offensive and kept pushing them back until they couldn't fight anymore. Foch also helped organize the peace agreement that ended the war, which was signed on a train.

Philippe Pétain - General

Known as the "Hero of Verdun," Pétain was a careful and organized leader who really cared for his soldiers. Even though the situation at Verdun seemed impossible, he helped bring order to the chaos and inspired his men to be brave.

Thanks to his leadership, the French troops played an important part in helping Ferdinand Foch's big attack in 1918, which helped push the war toward victory.

Pétain lost his good reputation in World War 2 when he became the leader of Vichy France, a government that worked with Nazi Germany. After the war, he was arrested and put in jail for betraying his country.

Italy

- **Victor Emmanuel III – King of Italy**

The Italian government didn't want to join the war, but King Victor overruled the government and sided with the Allies. He hoped to gain land from Austria-Hungary.

However, the Italian army wasn't very organized and had a lot of problems, leading to big losses. This caused Italy to go through a tough time, with many people struggling due to the economy.

- **Vittorio Orlando – Prime Minister**

Orlando became Prime Minister in 1917 and gave Italy hope after a big defeat at Caporetto. He was a strong supporter of the war and wanted the land the Allies had promised Italy in the Treaty of London in 1915. But when other leaders at the Paris Peace Conference didn't agree to give him what he wanted, he got upset and left the talks – this was one of the reasons that Italy fought on the side of Germany in WW2.

Belgium

- **King Albert I - King**

As the King of Belgium, Albert refused to let Germany pass through his country to get to France. Because of this, Germany invaded Belgium in 1914. When the German soldiers entered Belgium, Albert took charge of the army. However, the German forces were too strong, and he had to retreat.

Most of Belgium was occupied by Germany for the whole war. During this tough time, King Albert stayed close to his soldiers and visited them at the front lines to support them.

United States

Woodrow Wilson – President of USA

America stayed out of the war for a while because President Wilson believed that the country should remain neutral. However, he did ensure that America provided resources and funds to help.

It wasn't until 1917, when Germany began attacking merchant ships with submarines more often, that the United States felt it had to take action. Wilson convinced his government to join the war effort.

After the war ended, he played a key role in the peace talks and even suggested the idea of a League of Nations to help maintain peace.

Here are two of his most famous quotes about the war:

"This is a war to end all wars." The Daily News on August. 14, 1914

"I can predict with absolute certainty that within another generation there will be another world war if the nations of the world do not concert the method by which to prevent it" From a speech given at Omaha in 1919

- **General John Pershing – Commander in Chief of US Forces**

Nicknamed "Black Jack" and known as "Lord God Almighty" by the soldiers, Pershing was a legendary officer who inspired both respect and fear in his troops. In 1917, when the United States joined the war, President Wilson chose him to lead the AEF (Allied Expeditionary Force).

At first, Pershing focused on supporting the British and French armies by sending reinforcements to fill in gaps against the Germans.

But soon, he started leading his own troops and made a big difference by pushing back the Germans in battles at Catigny, Chateau-Thierry, and St. Mihiel.

- **DID YOU KNOW**
  - Douglas McArthur, who would go on to play a major role in WW2, was under Pershing's command during WW1 and impressed his commander as a second lieutenant.
  - During WWI, American hamburgers (named after the German city of Hamburg) were renamed **"liberty sandwiches"**. Frankfurters, named after Frankfurt in Germany, were called **"liberty sausages,"** and dachshunds became **"liberty dogs."** Schools stopped teaching German, and German-language books were burned.

Central Powers Political Leaders and Military Generals

Germany

Kaiser Wilhelm II – German Emperor

Wilhelm was the German emperor (Kaiser) and King of Prussia, and becoming ruler when he was just 29 years old. He wanted Germany to be strong and powerful and believed in building a strong army and navy, hoping to make Germany powerful, like Britain and France.

Kaiser Wilhelm was a key figure in the events that led to the war. He supported Austria-Hungary when they had declared was on Serbia/

He wasn't directly in charge of Germany's military plans, but as the emperor, he encouraged Germany's aggressive actions. He believed that his country could win the war quickly, but the conflict lasted much longer than anyone expected.

On November 9, 1918, as Germany was on the brink of losing the war, Kaiser Wilhelm stepped down (abdicated) as emperor and fled to the Netherlands to live in exile.

- ***DID YOU KNOW***

  - *As eldest grandchild of Britain's Queen Victoria,* ***Wilhelm was a cousin of the British King George V. King George was also a cousin of Tsar Nicholas****, making all three related. Wilhelm and Nicholas referred to each other as "**Willy**" and "**Nicky**," even when writing to each other, which makes it sound even more mad that we had a war between these countries!*

- **Erich Ludendorff - General**

Ludendorff was a very active leader who wanted a stronger army. At first, this made the leaders upset, and they gave him a smaller job. But when it seemed like Russia might defeat the 8th Army, he was promoted to be the second-in-command under General von Hindenburg. Together, they achieved a surprising victory at the Battle of Tannenberg in 1914. However, they faced a big defeat right after that at the Battle of Marne.

Hindenburg, Kaiser Wilhelm, and Ludendorff

By 1917, Ludendorff and von Hindenburg had gained full control of the army and were making important decisions for all of Germany. They even tried to find a new leader for the country.

Ludendorff allowed submarines to increase their attacks, which eventually led to the United States joining the war.

On March 21st, 1918, he attempted one last big attack against the Allies on the Western Front to defeat them before the Americans arrived, but it didn't work.

In the end, he resigned, claiming that his plans had been sabotaged by people in his own country.

- **Paul von Hindenburg – Field Marshall and Commander in Chief of Germany Army**

Not easily shaken, von Hindenburg became the leader of the German Army and gained fame for winning the Battle of Tannenberg. He was celebrated as a war hero for his efforts on the Eastern Front, but he didn't achieve the same success when fighting on the Western Front.

When it became clear that Germany was going to lose the war, he let Ludendorff take the blame for the defeats.

Later, he became the president of Germany and ran for a second term against a very ambitious Adolf Hitler.

Austria-Hungary

- **Emperor-King Franz Joseph I – Emperor of Austria, King of Hungary**

As the ruler of Austria-Hungary for 68 years, Franz Joseph had a lot of power in the region. He tried to keep peace by building friendships with other kings and emperors, but by the early 1900s, he didn't have many allies left, except for Wilhelm II of Germany.

Even though he believed in peace, he was convinced to give Serbia an ultimatum in 1914, which started a chain of declarations of war. He died in 1916.

- **Emperor-King Karl I (also know as Charles I of Austria)**

When he became king after Joseph I died, he quickly tried to make secret peace deals through his brother-in-law (with the rather grand name of Prince Sixtus von Bourbon-Parma, a Belgian officer in WWI), but France rejected them.

He also wanted to make changes to the Austro-Hungarian army, but it was too late because his country depended on Germany for military help.

As the war went on, he tried once more to find a peaceful solution, but it didn't work out. In the end, he had to give up his throne, and his empire was broken apart.

Ottoman Empire

- **Enver Pasha – Minister of War**

As the minister of war, he worked to create a military alliance with both Germany and Russia. When Russia turned down the proposals, he decided to join the Central Powers.

His first command of the Third Army was a big failure, suffering a tough defeat at Sarikamis on December 29th, 1914. But he later helped achieve a major victory at the Dardanelles. When the war ended, he escaped to Germany and then to Russia.

8. 1914 - MAJOR EVENTS & BATTLES

It's time to get stuck into the actual battles that took place in WWI and join the soldiers in their muddy trenches! Over the next few chapters, we'll look at the main battles that took place each year, who won each battle and at what cost in terms of injured and killed.

We'll be in France and Belgium, looking at events on The Western Front, across to Poland, Russia and Ukraine on The Eastern Front, as well as looking at events in Serbia, Turkey, Egypt and even in Asia. So, let's jump straight in!

We're going back to 1914, when World War 1 began. The battles that took place during this time set the stage for the long, hard war that was to come.

These early battles were full of brave soldiers, new and dangerous weapons, and difficult challenges.

Germany had a plan for war, called the Schlieffen Plan. It was named after a general and was based on a famous battle where Hannibal, a general from ancient times, defeated a much bigger Roman army. The plan was to attack and beat France quickly (Schlieffen thought it would take 6 weeks to defeat France!) while holding off Russia. Once France was defeated, the Germany would then turn its full attention to fighting Russia.

But, as often happens in war, things didn't go as planned! The war started on three fronts: Germany attacked Belgium and pushed toward France, Austria-Hungary fought Serbia, and Russia launched its own attack against Germany.

By the end of 1914, soldiers had dug trenches along both the Western and Eastern Fronts, and the war was far from over.

Siege of Liege

The quickest way for the Germans to reach Paris was to march straight through Belgium. They knew this might upset Britain, which promised to protect Belgium, but they took the risk anyway.

The Germans asked Belgium's king, Albert I, to let their army pass through peacefully, but the king refused, so the Germans invaded Belgium on August 4th.

The Germans expected an easy victory because they had more soldiers, but the Belgian army fought back harder than expected.

This brave resistance slowed down the Germans just enough for the Allies to gather their forces and defend Paris in time. The attack on Belgium was a big deal because it caused Britain to declare war on Germany!

Let's look at this invasion of Belgium in more detail.

August 5–16

The town of Liège, in Belgium, was very important because it was on the way to Paris and had railroads that the Germans could use to move their soldiers. But Liège was also one of the most heavily protected cities in Europe, with 12 strong forts surrounding it.

The German General, Otto von Emmich, wanted to take the city quickly, giving the German troops just two days to capture it. However, the Germans were not ready for how hard the Belgian soldiers would fight back.

On the first day, the Germans found that the Belgians had blown up all the bridges, making it hard to move forward. Instead of facing a weak army, the Germans realized the Belgians were much tougher than expected.

After the Belgians refused to surrender, the Germans started attacking the city but suffered more losses than expected. Erich von Ludendorff took command of the 14th Brigade, breaking through the eastern side of the city but still couldn't move forward without getting past the forts.

The Belgians continued to fight bravely. On August 7th, Ludendorff captured the Citadel of Liège, taking control of the city and two forts. The Germans brought in a giant cannon called a Krupp 420mm Howitzer to destroy the remaining forts, and by August 16th, the last two forts had fallen, forcing the Belgian army to retreat.

After Liege had fallen, the Germans continued their march through Belgium. They used the railways to move soldiers and supplies quickly and soon captured other Belgium cities such as Brussels and then finally crossed into France on August 24th.

Germany Loses Colonies

Fighting wasn't limited to Europe - other countries joined the battle to capture German colonies. In Africa, British and French forces easily captured Togoland, but Cameroon held out until February 1916. South African troops fought the Germans in German South – West Africa (Namibia) and won in July 1915.

In Asia, Jiaozhou (Kiaochow) Bay in China was taken by the Japanese, who then captured the important port of Tsingtao on November 7th, 1914.

In the Pacific, New Zealand troops took Western Samoa without a fight, and Australian forces captured New Guinea from the Germans after a short struggle. However, German East Africa (including present-day Rwanda, Burundi, and Tanzania) was different. The German forces there fought hard against Indian, British, and colonial troops. The fighting continued even after the war in Europe ended, and it wasn't until November 25th, 1918, that the German commander, Paul von Lettow-Vorbeck, finally surrendered.

These might seem like battles over unimportant territories, but the German resistance tied up almost 400,000 Allied soldiers who could have been fighting on the Western Front.

Serbian Campaign

WWI was not limited to trench warfare between Germany and the Allies. After all, it was Austria-Hungary's declaration of war on Serbia that kicked everything off, so let's take a look at what happened between Austria-Hungary and Serbia.

August 15–24

The Austrians bombed Belgrade, the capital of Serbia, and invaded with 200,000 soldiers, who were better equipped but smaller in number than the Serbian army. The Serbs were still recovering from earlier wars and some didn't even have boots!

After four days of fighting at Cer Mountain, the Serbs won on August 20th. The Austrians tried again at Šabac, but after another four days, the Serbs stood strong, even though they lost 40,000 men.

September 7–October 4

The Austrians launched another attack at the Drina River, crossing at night. The Serbs slowed them down long enough to get more help.

The battle turned into the first trench warfare of the war, with soldiers digging in for weeks.

The Serbs ran low on ammunition and could barely fight back as the Austrians kept bombarding them.

November 16–December 15

In their third invasion, the Austrians captured the city of Valjevo and pushed toward Belgrade. Both sides fought hard in heavy rain and snow. The Serbs were forced to retreat, and by November 25th, the Austrians reached the Kolubara River. But then, in a surprise counterattack, Serbia's soldiers forced the Austrians to retreat.

The Serbs were stretched thin and couldn't defend their capital, so the Austrians marched into Belgrade. On December 3rd, the Serb commander Putnik led another surprise attack, catching the Austrians off guard. The Serbs pushed them back across the Kolubara River and even out of the country.

The fighting cost Serbia dearly—170,000 soldiers were killed, captured, or injured—but it was still a victory. However, the Serbs knew it wouldn't be long before Austria-Hungary and its allies returned with an even bigger army.

Battle of the Frontiers

The Battle of the Frontiers was one of the first major military confrontations in World War I between Germany and France. It took place from August 7th to August 23rd, 1914, and consisted of a series of battles along the eastern border of France and in Belgium.

The Germans were pushing back the Belgian army and wanted to reach Paris quickly. On the other hand, France wanted to take back some land it had lost in earlier wars with its own plan, called Plan XVII.

August 7–26

The first French aim was to win back the cities of Mulhouse and Lorraine. They were successful at first, but soon the Germans came back and pushed them out again.

In the third battle, the French and German soldiers met in the thick fog of the Ardennes Forest. It started with a few small fights on August 21st, but things got much worse when the Germans used their powerful machine guns against the colourfully-dressed French soldiers who were charging at them.

Many soldiers from both sides were killed or injured, but the Germans were happy to dig in and start fighting from trenches, making the French retreat.

The last two battles saw the Germans making the first move. The first was at Charleroi, where both sides fought very hard, but the French were outnumbered and had to fall back.

The final battle was at Mons, where British troops, called the British Expeditionary Force (BEF), arrived to help the French. The commander of the BEF, John French, sent his 75,000 soldiers against a German army that was twice as big on August 23rd. Unfortunately, the British were outnumbered and had to retreat, losing 1,600 men while the Germans lost 5,000.

These defeats were a big wake-up call for the Allies, reminding them that they needed to work together to face the challenges ahead.

Even though the Germans won most of the battles during this period, the Allies regrouped. This set the stage for the First Battle of the

Marne, where the Allies stopped the German advance in September 1914.

WW1 trench

Battle of Tannenberg

Now we travel to the Eastern Front, and the first battle between Russia and Germany.

The Battle of Tannenberg was important because it took place in a location where a big battle had happened 500 years earlier during the Teutonic Wars, and the Germans had lost back then. They really wanted to win this time! But we know that the German plan was to focus on France first and then turn their attention to Russia.

However, the Russians didn't stick to the German plan and decided to attack first! They had many more soldiers than the Germans, which gave them an advantage. But things changed when the Germans discovered that they could listen in on Russian communications.

August 26–30

The Russians launched a successful attack with their First and Second Armies. At first, it seemed like they were winning, and the Germans began to fall back. To turn things around, two German leaders, Paul von Hindenburg and Erich von Ludendorff, were called in to help. They reorganized the German army and used trains to bring in more soldiers and supplies.

By intercepting radio messages, the Germans realized that the Russian armies were too far apart to support each other. They decided to focus their attack on the Second Army. On August 26th, the Germans surprised the Russians, and within two days, the Russians were forced to retreat. Some Russian soldiers got so scared that they dropped their weapons and ran, but many were trapped!

The Russian commander, Samsonov, felt so defeated that he took his own life. Although it's hard to know the exact numbers, it's believed that around 120,000 to 170,000 Russian soldiers were either killed or wounded, while the Germans lost about 13,000.

This was a huge defeat for the larger Russian army, and both von Hindenburg and von Ludendorff became heroes in Germany. Even though the battle happened near a different city (now called Olsztyn in Poland), it was named the Battle of Tannenberg as a way for the Germans to get revenge for their loss 500 years earlier.

First Battle of the Marne

We've arrived back in France and the Western Front! This battle was a crucial victory for the Allies who had been on the run in almost every meeting with the Germans up until that point. By stopping the

German forces from advancing any further, they saved France from falling into the enemy's hands.

The Battle of the Marne is often remembered as one of the most important battles of World War I, as it changed the course of the war and set the stage for the years of trench warfare that followed.

September 6–12

Following the Schlieffen Plan, the Germans made a strong push towards Paris. The Allied forces were tired from fighting and had to keep retreating, so it looked like the Germans might win.

As Paris prepared for an attack, thinking the city would soon be surrounded, General Joseph Joffre, the French commander, decided to fight back. On September 6th, he launched a counterattack with the help of the British Expeditionary Force led by John French.

As the Germans turned to face the attack, they accidentally created a big gap between their troops—about 30 miles wide! The BEF rushed through this opening, taking the Germans by surprise.

Although the Allies had the element of surprise, they still needed more help. The next day, 6,000 reinforcements arrived in 600 taxis and buses from Paris, which helped keep their momentum going.

On the evening of September 7th, the Allies launched another surprise attack that widened the gap even more. By September 9th, the Germans started to retreat. They reached the River Aisne and dug trenches, preparing for a long battle ahead.

In total, about two million soldiers fought in this battle. The French suffered about 250,000 casualties, while the Germans had a similar number, and the British lost around 12,733 soldiers.

The Schlieffen Plan, which aimed to fight only one war at a time, had failed. Now, the Germans were forced to fight on both the Eastern and Western Fronts!

- **DID YOU KNOW**
    - *Reconnaissance planes were used for the first time at Marne by the Allies to spot military positions from the air and use that information to help win the battle on the ground.*

Church in Laventie, France, wrecked by German bombs

First Battle of Ypres

Ypres, along with Verdun, The Somme and Passchendaele, are places and battles that have become infamous for the brutal conditions, enormous suffering of soldiers and the almost pointlessness of the battles that occurred in those places, where so many died for so little gain.

Once both sides settled into trench warfare, the only way to defeat the enemy was to outflank them, which means to go around their army. This led to what was called the "Race to the Sea", where both the Allies and the Germans tried to be the first to reach the North Sea, and cut off supply lines and stop the enemy's movement.

The last place where this was possible was Ypres, a small city on the coast of Belgium.

October 19–November 22 The British Expeditionary Force arrived in Ypres, and their leader, Field Marshal John French, decided to team up with the French commander, Ferdinand Foch, to launch an attack. But before they could act, the German army chief, Falkenhayn, started an attack on October 20th that threatened to break through the Belgian defenses.

On October 27th, King Albert I of Belgium ordered the sluice gates holding back the North Sea to be opened, flooding a twenty-mile area of land and stopping the Germans in their tracks.

Falkenhayn then turned his focus to attacking the city of Ypres itself with a cavalry charge. However, the British soldiers were so quick and precise with their rifles that the Germans thought they were facing machine guns, and they were driven back.

Another attack took place on November 11th, but the Germans were slow to take advantage, and a British unit made up of cooks, medical orderlies, and engineers pushed the Germans back again.

The fighting was intense and confusing, leading to 150,000 Allied and 130,000 German soldiers getting hurt or killed. Only the cold winter weather eventually brought the battle to an end.

The battle ended in a stalemate, and the front lines became firmly fixed, leading to a prolonged period of trench warfare.

Christmas Truce

December 24–25

Thankfully we can now talk about a happy event in the midst of a horrible war! At Christmas, something special happened along the Western Front.

Some soldiers decided to call an unofficial truce, which means they took a break from fighting to celebrate the holiday. While some soldiers continued to fight, others came out of their trenches to meet their enemies. They exchanged gifts, sang Christmas carols, and even played friendly soccer games in no-man's-land, the empty area between the two sides.

British and German troops. Christmas 1914

One German soldier's diary said:

The English brought a soccer ball from the trenches, and pretty soon a lively game ensued. How marvelously wonderful, yet how strange it was. The English officers felt the same way about it. Thus Christmas, the celebration of Love, managed to bring mortal enemies together as friends for a time.

Another British officer wrote:

At 8.30 I fired three shots in the air and put up a flag with "Merry Christmas" on it, and I climbed on the parapet. The Germans put up a sheet with "Thank you" on it, and the German captain appeared on the parapet. We both bowed and saluted and got down into our respective trenches, and he fired two shots in the air, and the War was on again.

All British soldiers received packages from Princess Mary, King George V's daughter. In the metal boxes were chocolates and butterscotch, cigarettes and tobacco, a picture of Mary, and a greeting from the king.

In the middle of the madness of war, it was a moment of kindness and fun and a recognition by many soldiers that the enemy was just like them…ordinary people, with loved ones at home, who had been dragged into a fight!

9. 1915 - MAJOR EVENTS & BATTLES

In 1915, World War I continued to be a brutal and intense conflict with significant battles. The Western Front was at a stalemate, despite all the different tactics used from gas attacks to the "creeping barrage," but this resulted only in heavy casualties with very little to show for it.

In other regions, the Germans achieved a number of significant breakthroughs which strengthened the belief that the Central Powers could win the war.

The Allies, however, achieved few victories, and the British were even forced to make changes to its government to try and find a new direction.

Gallipoli

We're off to Turkey this time, to the Gallipoli Campaign.

The Allies wanted to capture the Gallipoli Peninsula to secure a sea route to Russia and knock the Ottoman Empire out of the war. The campaign, which lasted from February 1915 to January 1916, ended in failure, resulting in heavy casualties for both sides and was one of the most disastrous Allied efforts of the entire war.

With the Western Front not showing any signs of shifting, those in charge began looking for other areas where they could make an impact and change the course of the war by knocking out one of the Central Powers.

One option was the Dardanelles, a narrow waterway connecting the Mediterranean Sea to the Black Sea. It was also the route to Constantinople, the capital of the Ottoman Empire. Winston Churchill had a bold idea to use the navy to break through, but the ships faced trouble from mines in the water and were easily targeted. So, the Allies decided to shift from a sea invasion to a land attack.

Australian troops resting in Egypt before the Gallipoli campaign

February 17, 1915 – January 9, 1916

From February 17th, 1915, to January 9th, 1916, the Allies planned to take control of the Gallipoli Peninsula, which guarded the Dardanelles Strait.

With a mix of British, French, Irish, Indian, Australian, and New Zealand troops, they had nearly 489,000 soldiers, while the Ottomans had around 315,000 soldiers, under the command of General Otto Liman von Sanders.

The Turkish army had already spent six weeks preparing for an assault, and the Allied attack came as no surprise to them.

The Allies made their first landing at Cape Helles on April 25th, but it was poorly managed, and they suffered heavy losses, even though they eventually got through. The second landing, by the ANZACs (Australian and New Zealand Army Corps), went a bit better.

However, by April 28th, progress came to a halt, and both sides dug trenches, leading to the very situation the Allies had wanted to avoid! The conditions were terrible: the heat made it hard to fight, food was spoiled, and flies swarmed over the dead bodies.

After many failed attempts to break the deadlock, a new commander was installed and immediately called for an evacuation.

After almost a year of fighting without any significant achievements, the Gallipoli Campaign was a complete failure. The Allies suffered 187,959 casualties, while the Turks had 161,828. As a result, Churchill lost his position, and the British government was blamed for the disaster.

- *DID YOU KNOW*
  - *About **50,000 Australians** served at Gallipoli during the campaign. Out of these, around **8,700** lost their lives,*
  - *The Gallipoli campaign is considered a significant moment in Australian history because it helped shape the country's national identity and spirit. The bravery of the ANZACs is commemorated on **ANZAC day** every year on April 25th, and their story continues to inspire Australians today.*

Australians and British soldier in Egypt

Second Battle of Ypres

We're back in Ypres once again, on The Western Front! The Allies created a protective area around the city of Ypres called the Ypres Salient, but the German soldiers had the advantage of higher ground. After trying to take Ypres the year before, the Germans launched another attack in 1915, hoping to distract the Allies from their movements in the east.

Ruined town of Ypres

April 22–May 25

The German commander, Falkenhayn, wanted to attack to distract the Allies from noticing the German troop movements in the east.

As part of this diversion, he ordered the use of a dangerous new weapon: chlorine gas. On April 22nd, they released gas from 5,000 canisters near Gravenstafel Ridge, and it caught the French soldiers off guard, causing many to choke and flee. About 6,000 French soldiers died in just one hour!

The fighting continued fiercely, with Canadian soldiers trying to protect themselves with soaked handkerchiefs, but they still had to retreat.

Although the Allies lost some ground, they managed to hold onto Ypres. In the end, there were about 70,000 Allied casualties, which was double the number of German casualties.

- *DID YOU KNOW*
    - *The Germans used poison gas for the first time in warfare during the Second Battle of Ypres. This tactic caused panic and severe casualties among the troops.*
    - *Canadian officer, John McRae, who was at this battle near Flanders, wrote one of the most well-known war poems for his friend who died there. Here is an excerpt:*

In Flanders fields the poppies blow
Between the crosses, row on row,
That mark our place; and in the sky
The larks, still bravely singing, fly
Scarce heard amid the guns below.
We are the Dead. Short days ago
We lived, felt dawn, saw sunset glow,
Loved and were loved, and now we lie.

- *WW1 produced other notable poets, including Wilfred Owens, who wrote the line, "it is sweet and fitting to die for one's country". Siegfried Sassoon wrote over 100 anti-war poems, vividly describing the horrors of what he had seen. He was recognized for his bravery on the battlefield and nicknamed "Mad Jack" for his courage.*

Gorlice-Tarnow Offensive

Fighting continued on The Eastern Front in 1915, and this battle was the first time Austria-Hungary and Germany had combined forces, with a successful outcome.

It was originally designed as a small offensive to relieve Russian pressure on the Austro-Hungarians. However, not only did the Central Powers win a surprising and quick victory, but they managed to deal a huge blow to the Russian army, forcing them to retreat deep into Russian territory.

This was surprising because the Schlieffen Plan expected a quick win against France and a long fight with the Russians. Instead, things turned out very differently in 1915!

May 2–July 13

The attack started with a huge barrage of artillery and 40,000 soldiers going against the Russians near Poland. This helped the Central Powers move 10 kilometers forward on the very first day! Even though the Russians tried to bring in more soldiers to help, they couldn't stop the advancing troops.

Within just eight days, the Russian army fell apart, and the leaders ordered them to retreat. Around 100,000 Russian soldiers were either killed or hurt, and another 250,000 were captured and morale was broken.

The Central Powers had a big victory on the Eastern Front, but for some reason, they didn't use this winning strategy of combining armies again!

Battle of Loos

Back on The Western Front, the Battle of Loos took place in northern France, near Lens. This battle is notable for the British using poison gas for the first time, releasing 140 tons of chlorine gas.

After some big losses, the Allies wanted to win a battle. Joseph Joffre, the French leader, decided to try again to take back the Artois region, which he had tried to capture twice before without success. He planned a two-part attack: while the French soldiers headed to Souchez, he asked the British to capture the town of Loos. Unfortunately, this battle would not go well for the Allies because the Germans had better defenses.

September 25–October 8

British commander John French asked General Douglas Haig to lead the attack, but Haig was worried because they didn't have enough heavy guns or shells, and the open land made it hard to march. However, they attacked anyway.

The British began their attack with chlorine gas, but the wind blew the gas back towards them, causing 2,632 British soldiers to be hurt instead. Even so, they managed to take the village of Loos, but they had to wait for more soldiers to arrive while the Germans reinforced their defenses.

Town of Lille completely destroyed

Before the attack, the British fired over 250,000 shells at the German trenches to weaken them, but this just warned the Germans that an attack was coming.

On September 26th, the British moved forward in groups without any artillery support, but they quickly lost half their soldiers to German machine gun fire. The Germans decided to stop firing and let the remaining British soldiers retreat.

The battle continued with a failed German counterattack to take back Loos, and the British tried another gas attack that didn't work either.

In the end, the British had very few gains but suffered 50,000 casualties, while the Germans lost about half that number. This failure was a big reason why John French was replaced by General Haig as the British commander.

Siege of Kut

Just when you think the British have enough on their plate in fighting in France, they were also fighting in Iraq, against the Ottomans! After all, it was called a 'World' War! Let's take a look at what was going on here.

At the end of a tough year for the Allies, the French tried several times to take back strongholds from the Germans in Champagne, France, but they had no success. Many soldiers had been killed or hurt, and there was little to show for their efforts. The British were also recovering from heavy losses.

Another disappointment was that the Ottomans were not as easy to defeat as everyone had hoped. While the British focused mainly on the Western Front, they were also stretched thinly in Iraq, trying to control the area and stop a Muslim uprising. This situation was just another challenge for the Allies during a difficult time.

Machine Gun Corps. Gaza Line

December 3–April 29, 1916

Major General Charles Townshend led the Indian Expeditionary Force (IEF), which included both British and Indian soldiers. They had tried to capture Baghdad from the Ottomans but were unsuccessful.

On November 25th, Townshend and his 15,000 men retreated 100 miles to a city called Kut al-Amara. The Ottomans surrounded the city and tried to take it several times, but when those attacks failed, they set up a siege instead.

New soldiers came to help, but they were inexperienced and tried four times to rescue the trapped troops, suffering over 23,000 casualties each time.

Efforts to send help by submarines and planes also didn't work, and the soldiers inside Kut grew weaker as their food ran out. After 147 days, Townshend began talks with the Ottoman commander, Halil, even offering bribes of one million and then two million pounds, but they were refused.

Eventually, Townshend had to surrender, and he and his 13,000 became prisoners. Sadly, about 70% of the men died while marching to prison camps or during their time in captivity.

Although this defeat didn't change the war's outcome or affect the British Empire much, it was still one of its biggest losses. Halil, the Ottoman commander, said it was a Turkish victory *"the likes of which hadn't been seen for 200 years."*

10. 1916 - MAJOR EVENTS & BATTLES

As World War I entered its third year, there was still no clear winner or loser. Both sides had experienced heavy losses, but neither had made any big advances to turn the tide of the war.

Despite the many lives lost, there wasn't much to show for it – little territory had been captured. However, the commanders were eager to prove themselves.

The Allies were planning a major summer attack along the River Somme in France, while the Germans were preparing to lure their enemies into a big battle at Verdun. These two battles would turn out to be the longest and bloodiest of the entire war.

Meanwhile, the Russians were making new plans to fight back against the Germans, and the Italians were continuing their skirmishes along the Isonzo River against Austria-Hungary.

Once again, it was another tough year of fighting!

Battle of Verdun

This battle lasted almost a year and was one of the deadliest in World War I. The Germans planned to wear down the French by attacking them continuously, hoping that the heavy losses would force the French to ask for peace.

They were successful in causing many casualties and tiring out their opponents. However, the French didn't give up, and finally forced the Germans to retreat, bringing the battle to an end.

Wounded British, French and Italian soldiers

February 21–December 18

The fortress town of Verdun, located on the River Meuse, was very important because it protected the nearby plains and a route to Paris. German Commander Erich von Falkenhayn planned a big battle there and took seven weeks to prepare. He had to wait to start because of bad weather, which gave the French time to get ready.

On the first day of the battle, the Germans began with a 10-hour bombardment. They used special soldiers called stormtroopers, who had grenades and machine guns, along with soldiers with flamethrowers, to push the French back three miles. General Philippe Petain took charge of the French army and worked hard to strengthen the city's defenses to slow the German advance.

In a nearby village called Douaumont, the Germans faced heavy fire and had to change their plans. Instead of attacking head-on, they started to target the sides of the city. They were pushed back by strong French resistance. The Germans bombed Fort Vaux, day and night, until they finally captured it.

Desperate for help, the French asked the British to start their offensive at the Somme sooner than planned, which worked! The Germans had to pull some soldiers away from Verdun to deal with this new threat.

The Russians also started attacking on the Eastern Front, and Germany scrambled to send reinforcements there. With the battle at a standstill, Falkenhayn was replaced in August by Field Marshal Paul von Hindenburg.

In October, General Robert Nivelle of the French army began using heavy artillery to attack the Germans near Verdun. By November, both Fort Vaux and Douaumont were back in French hands. The Germans suffered over 430,000 casualties, while the French lost around 500,000 soldiers.

Although a victory for the French, they would not forget this battle. At the end of the war, they forced has terms on Germany in the Treaty of Versailles, as punishment for what happened during the war.

- *DID YOU KNOW*

    - *Because many of the soldiers were buried by explosions or could not be identified, their remains were placed in the Douaumont Ossuary, a memorial that* **holds 130,000 French and German soldiers' remains**.

    - *French and German armies fired between* **40 and 60 million artillery shells**. *About* **10 million unexploded shells are still in the soil** *around Verdun, and bomb squads are still removing 40 tons each year.*

- ○ ***Nine villages near Verdun were completely destroyed*** *during the battle, and have never been rebuilt.*

Battle of Jutland

Let's go to sea!

Before the war, the Germans and British were trying to build the biggest navies, but there were not as many battles at sea as on land. The Battle of Jutland was the only big fight between their battleships.

WWI battleship

May 31–June 1

To break the blockade set by the Allies, German Vice Admiral Reinhard Scheer wanted to trap half of the British Royal Navy fleet and then fight the rest. He planned to lure Vice Admiral David Beatty's Battlecruiser Fleet into a trap where his High Seas Fleet would be waiting. However, British codebreakers intercepted the plans, so they sent both Beatty and Admiral John Jellicoe to meet the Germans instead.

When the two sides met near Denmark, there was a chaotic battle. The Germans struck first by damaging Beatty's main ship, HMS Lion, and sinking two others, HMS Indefatigable and HMS Queen Mary. Although Beatty fired some shots, none were powerful enough to sink an enemy ship, and he had to retreat until Jellicoe arrived.

Once the entire Royal Navy Fleet was together against the High Seas Fleet, intense fighting broke out. Many ships were hit, and some were damaged, while others tried to escape.

When Jellicoe chased after Scheer, the German admiral used smoke to cover his retreat, realizing he didn't have enough power to fight back. As night fell, there was more chaotic fighting as the British tried to block Scheer from escaping, but due to clever maneuvers and miscommunication, he managed to slip away. By dawn, he was too far to be caught.

The battle involved 250 ships and 100,000 men, with the British losing 14 ships and the Germans losing 11. Although the Germans avoided being completely defeated, they never again seriously challenged British control of the North Sea.

Brusilov Offensive

Back on land, we're zooming around again, this time to The Eastern Front!

The Russians had not done very well in the war so far, suffering several defeats on the Eastern Front. Even though they had many more soldiers than their enemy, they made too many mistakes and weren't poorly organized. They really needed a victory, and General Aleksei Brusilov had a plan to help them win one!

His strategy worked so well that Austria-Hungary couldn't take part in any further battles for the rest of the war!

June 4–August 10

The battle took place in Galicia, in modern-day north-western Ukraine. General Brusilov wanted to surprise the Austrians with a strong attack, so he prepared his soldiers well by training them using large-scale models.

When they met the enemy on June 4th, the Austrians were shocked by how powerful and accurate the Russian soldiers were. Using 2,000 cannons to bombard a 200-mile-long front, the Russians quickly defeated their opponents, capturing 26,000 soldiers in just one day!

In only two days, they advanced an amazing 75 kilometers, which was more than any other army had done in the war.

To help the Austrians, the Germans had to step in, which weakened its defenses at Verdun, allowing the French to gain the upper hand there.

The damage to the Austro-Hungarian army was so severe that it could no longer be a major force in the war.

Casualties, once again, were huge - in total, Austria-Hungary lost between 1 million and 1.5 million soldiers who were killed, wounded, or captured, while the Russians lost between 500,000 and 1 million.

Battle of the Somme

We're now returning to France for the Battle of the Somme. This was one of the bloodiest battles in history and one of the largest battles in WWI with over 1 million soldiers killed or wounded.

For many in Britain, the battle remains the most painful and infamous episode of the First World War.

Fought along the Somme River in France, it was a joint operation between British and French armies, designed to wear down the enemy with heavy bombings and attacks. The commanders knew there would be many deaths on both sides, but they were willing to accept these losses as long as they hurt the enemy more.

In the end, very little land was gained to justify the huge number of soldiers lost. Although the battle weakened the German army, many people see it as a tragic and unnecessary loss of life.

Cheshire Regiment in Somme trench

July 1–November 13

General Douglas Haig had big plans for the Battle of the Somme, but the officers struggled to get everything ready in time, especially when the start date was moved up to help the French at Verdun. This was all part of the "Big Push," a plan for the Russians, French, Italians, and British to attack at the same time to end the war.

A week before the battle, the British fired 1.5 million shells at the German defenses, hoping to clear a path for the soldiers. But many of the shells didn't explode, missed their targets, or failed to damage the strong German bunkers.

On July 1, 1916th, British troops rushed across No Man's Land to fight, but found the barbed wire and defenses still standing. The Germans came out of their hiding places and opened fire, killing 19,000 and injuring 38,000 in just one day! It was a terrible loss for the British.

In the days that followed, more attacks took place. Each attack was planned better than the one before, as the officers learned from their earlier mistakes. On July 14th, the Allies surprised the Germans and captured Longueval Ridge. But even with this success, they didn't get the big breakthrough they were hoping for, and the fighting became stuck again.

There were a total of 12 different battles, with the Germans fighting back each time.

By September, the battle was still going on along the front lines. The British introduced 32 new Mark I tanks. At first, these tanks surprised the Germans because they had never seen them before. But the tanks were slow and hard to move around, which made them easy targets, and many were destroyed.

Then the autumn rains came, and the ground turned to thick mud. The soldiers found it hard to move, the attack lost its momentum and came to an end.

Many people wondered if all the fighting at the Somme had been worth it. General Haig, who was in charge of the British forces, was even nicknamed the "Butcher of the Somme" because so many soldiers had died under his command.

The number of soldiers killed or wounded was enormous: about 420,000 British, 200,000 French, and around 450,000 Germans.

Marching towards the Battle of the Somme

- **DID YOU KNOW**

  ○ ***No Man's Land*** *is the space that lies between the trenches of two sides in a battle. This area was very **dangerous for soldiers** because it was exposed to enemy fire. It was usually muddy, filled with barbed wire, and littered with the remains of equipment and sometimes even soldiers who couldn't make it back to safety.*

  ○ *To motivate his men, Captain Wilfred "Billie" Nevill **promised a prize to the first person who kicked a football into German trenches** as they advanced. Some troops came into no-man's-land with footballs and a cheer, but they were cut down minutes later.*

  ○ *On the first day of the battle, the British suffered horrendous casualties—over 57,470, with 19,240 killed—mak-*

ing it the **bloodiest day in British military history**.

- *A full-length film called "The Battle of the Somme" was seen by over 20 million people after it came out in August 1916. Instead of boosting morale, many were upset by what they saw.*

- **Adolf Hitler injured his leg at the Somme** *after shrapnel from an explosive went off near him. He was also involved in the First Battle of Ypres and later at Passchendaele.*

11. 1917 - MAJOR EVENTS & BATTLES

After the intense battles of 1916, both sides were trying to recover and see how many soldiers they had left to send into the fight on both the Western and Eastern Fronts.

The Allies were growing stronger, with 3.9 million soldiers compared to Germany's 2.5 million. Because they had more troops, the Allies were ready to go on the attack.

In response, German leaders Ludendorff and von Hindenburg decided to pull back to stronger defensive lines and focus on holding their ground.

Meanwhile, Russia was having big problems at home. The Bolshevik Revolution overthrew Tsar Nicholas, causing chaos in the country. At the same time, the United States entered the war, which made a huge difference and changed the course of the conflict.

Vimy Ridge

As part of a bigger plan by the new French leader, General Nivelle, the goal was to take Vimy Ridge, a high point that overlooked both Arras and Artois. This would give the Allies a big advantage. The Canadian Corps was given the difficult task, after the French had already tried and lost 100,000 men.

Canadian troops following Mark II tank Vimy Ridge

April 9–12

The Canadians trained for weeks, forming special groups of soldiers and digging tunnels to get close to the enemy. For seven days before the attack, artillery guns fired accurately to weaken German defenses. Their leader, Julian Byng, told the soldiers, "You must go forward exactly on time, like a train, or you will be destroyed." With 1,000 artillery guns helping, 15,000 Canadians stormed the ridge, even though it was snowing, capturing key positions in just 30 minutes. They even charged at the last machine gun nests using bayonets!

The Canadians lost over 3,000 men, with around 7,000 wounded, but it was a major victory for them.

- **DID YOU KNOW**
  - In 1922, **the French gave Vimy Ridge to Canada**, as a

reward for the incredible sacrifice they made. A memorial stands there now as a reminder of the Canadians' courage.

Messines

Staying on The Western Front, this battle was all about capturing the 250-foot-high ridge of Messines near Ypres. The Germans had held onto it for a long time, giving them a big advantage. Instead of charging at the Germans, the plan was to surprise them with one of the biggest explosions ever!

June 7–14

For over a year, soldiers from Britain, Canada and Australia had been secretly digging tunnels under the German trenches. Some tunnels were over a mile long and 300 feet (91m) deep! It was a very dangerous job, and some lost their lives when tunnels collapsed. But by June, the soldiers had filled the tunnels with 600 tons of explosives.

At 3am, the biggest man-made explosion in history went off, killing 10,000 German soldiers and completely destroying the town. It was so huge that it changed the entire landscape!

By 7am, New Zealand soldiers, helped by artillery fire as they advanced, had taken control of Messines.

Major General Charles Harington was right when he said, "I don't know if we'll change history tomorrow, but we'll certainly change the geography."

- **DID YOU KNOW**
  - *The explosion was considered the* **loudest man-made**

noise in history, and was ***heard in London!*** *It left a crater 145 ft (44m) deep and 380 ft (115m) wide, some of which is still visible today.*

- *The British also built **decoy tunnels** to divert the attention of the German miners. The Germans detonated charges to collapse the decoy tunnels, thinking they had defused the threat.*

- *Most of the **WW1 tunnelers had been miners** before the war. It was dangerous and stressful work, but miners knew how to handle tough conditions underground, like poor air quality and the danger of tunnels collapsing.*

- *Soldiers dug **over 100 miles** of tunnels along the Western Front!*

Third Battle of Ypres

Yes, again, we're back at Ypres in Belgium!

Also known as Passchendaele, this battle has played a big role in how people think about World War 1. It showed just how difficult and terrible the war had become, with so many soldiers stuck in the mud, and so many lives lost for very little gain.

General Haig wanted to defeat the Germans around Ypres once and for all, hoping to end the long-lasting deadlock in the area.

After the huge success at Messines, the British were very confident and decided to go all out in their attack.

But heavy rain made everything muddy, and in the end, the battle didn't accomplish much—except causing a lot of lives to be lost.

WW1 artillery

July 31–November 6

The British fired 4.5 million shells from 3,000 guns at the German lines, but this wasn't enough to destroy the strong concrete shelters where German machine guns were hidden.

The rain and explosions turned the battlefield into thick mud, making it extremely difficult for soldiers and tanks to move forward. Even though it was a disaster, Haig told his men to keep going, leading to 70,000 British soldiers being hurt or killed.

One small victory came when the Canadians managed to capture the town of Lens, but the rest of the fighting was stuck. Haig was told to stop, but when the weather improved, he ordered more attacks.

Using a "creeping barrage," the Allies started to make progress. Haig thought the Germans were about to collapse, so he launched more attacks in October. But then the rain came back, the mud returned, and the new attacks failed to change anything.

It turned into a nightmare! Even the beautiful nature that once covered the area had been completely destroyed. As Private R.A. Colwell said:

There was not a sign of life of any sort. Not a tree, save for a few dead stumps which looked strange in the moonlight. Not a bird, not even a rat or a blade of grass. Nature was as dead as those Canadians whose bodies remained where they had fallen the previous autumn. Death was written large everywhere.

While trying to capture Passchendaele Ridge, soldiers struggled in terrible conditions. They hid in muddy, water-filled craters as rain poured down and explosions shook the ground. Many got lost trying to return to their camps, and their rifles often stopped working in the wet conditions. Stretcher-bearers had to walk through deep mud to help the wounded.

After capturing just a few high points, General Haig finally called off the attack. Both sides suffered huge losses—270,000 on the Allied side and 220,000 for the Germans.

In the end, nothing important was gained, and the battle only brought more death.

- ***DID YOU KNOW***
  - *In 1918, during the Spring Offensive led by the Germans, instead of trying to defend the Passchendaele Ridge, the* **British gave it up without firing one shot!**

- *Creeping barrage was a tactic that involved using artillery to create a **slow-moving wall of fire that infantry followed behind** – it created a protective barrier for soldiers to follow. It kept the enemy under cover until the infantry was close enough to attack.*

Battle of Cambrai

The Battle of Cambrai was different from other battles because of the new methods and equipment used. For the first time ever, the British launched a full-scale tank attack with a special tank division.

At first, they made good progress and took ground from the Germans, but later lost it again. Even though they didn't keep the land, this battle changed how modern wars would be fought by showing how powerful tanks could be.

American WW1 tank

November 20–December 5

With over 400 Mark VI tanks, each carrying a crew of eight and moving at 6 km/h, the British made a strong push into enemy territory. This was a big improvement from the first-time tanks were used, showing just how powerful they could be when used correctly. Working together with artillery and soldiers on foot, the attack was very successful at the start.

However, problems soon arose. By the end of the first day, only half of the tanks were still working because of mechanical issues or being hit by enemy artillery.

The Germans, known for quickly sending in reinforcements, strengthened their defenses. They launched a counterattack, and the British lost much of the land they had just taken. This battle made the Germans believe they were strong enough to defeat the Allies before the Americans joined the war.

12. 1918 - MAJOR EVENTS & BATTLES

When Russia left the war in March 1918, the British knew the Germans would focus all their strength on the Western Front, trying to win before the United States joined in. The British plan wasn't to attack but to defend, hoping to hold out long enough for the new American troops to arrive.

Germany launched the Spring Offensive, its last major attack, in a desperate attempt to break through the trenches and defeat Britain and France while they still could. But once the Americans arrived, the tide quickly turned against Germany and the Central Powers.

Fresh soldiers and supplies strengthened the Allies, who switched from defense to offense in a series of battles that led to the war's end.

At the same time, U.S. President Woodrow Wilson played a key role in pushing for peace.

Spring Offensive

Germany's General Ludendorff planned a series of attacks to break apart the British and French forces. He divided it into five main phases, with each part targeting specific goals. The idea was to succeed before the Americans fully joined the fight.

However, Ludendorff made a big mistake. He thought the British and French were weak and stuck in their trenches, but they fought back harder than he expected. This resistance made it much tougher for the Germans than they had planned.

WWI German A7V Tank (Sturmpanzerwagen in German)

Operation Michael: March 21–April 5

Sometimes called the Second Battle of the Somme, this attack began with huge artillery fire, gas, and smoke screens. Five hours later, German infantry advanced. Using fog for cover, the stormtroopers surprised the enemy, and the defensive line was pushed back.

Ludendorff's men won several battles and captured 1196 square miles (3,100 square kilometers) of land, but none of it was very useful.

The Germans moved so fast that they ended up far from their supply lines and had to slow down to let supplies catch up. This gave the Allies enough time to bring in reinforcements and slow the Germans down even more.

After a few days, the offensive lost momentum and was called off. Even though the British defenses were pushed hard, they never broke.

- **DID YOU KNOW**
    - *In the first day of battle over **3 million rounds of artillery** were used, with **1.1 million being used in the first 5 hours!** This was as many as the British fired in a week at the Battle of the Somme in 1916!*

Operation Georgette: April 9–29

This next phase aimed to capture the important rail hub at Hazebrouk, which would help the Germans take the port and cut off the troops guarding Ypres. They launched a strong attack that hit the Allies hard enough to force them to collapse and retreat.

The Germans reclaimed Messines and the Passchendaele Ridge, stretching the British defenses along the River Lys. If Ludendorff had launched another strong push, he could have broken through to the port just 15 miles away!

However, he spread out his attack and lost momentum. On top of that, there were logistical problems that slowed the Germans down, and the offensive ended without capturing Hazebrouk.

Operation Blücher–Yorck: May 27–July 18

In this part of the Spring Offensive, the Germans aimed to draw French troops away from the coast and split the Allied forces. Their initial attack was successful, breaking through the frontlines and opening a path to the River Marne, which was just 90 miles from Paris. The French government was so worried about losing the city that they ordered an evacuation.

At this point, American troops arrived and recaptured important locations like Cantigy, Vaux, and Belleau Wood. This was a big boost for the Allies, who had been struggling during the German offensive. However, Ludendorff stretched his forces too thin, spreading his troops across a large area.

Operation Gneisenau: June 9–12

In the fourth phase of the offensive, the Germans hoped to make big gains and connect their territory with Amiens. However, the French had learned about the attack from prisoners they captured and were ready to fight back.

On June 11th, the French launched a strong counterattack without any warning. The Germans were surprised, as there had been no initial bombardment to signal the attack.

Facing 150 tanks and four French divisions, Ludendorff's plans came to a halt once again.

Second Battle of the Marne: July 15–18

The last German attack was called Operation Friedensturm. General Ludendorff wanted to distract troops from Flanders, where he had plans for another attack later. This time, however, the Germans faced a tough start because the French had built fake trenches along the front lines, tricking them.

Although the Germans managed to cross the Marne River, a quick counterattack pushed them back, and they lost much of the ground they had gained in the previous phase.

This was a crucial defeat that marked the end of the German offensives. From that point on, the momentum shifted to the Allies.

Battle of Amiens

This battle was the first in what became known as the Hundred Days Offensive. After seeing the confusion in the German forces following the Second Battle of the Marne, Marshal Ferdinand Foch suggested that the Allies target important places like the Amiens railway junction.

The Allies learned from their past mistakes and used better strategies, combining flexible infantry with tanks and aircraft. This cooperation overwhelmed the Germans and led to one of their worst defeats.

August 8–12

Secretly, the Allies put together a massive force for the battle, which included 500 tanks, 1,900 airplanes, 2,000 artillery pieces, and a large number of soldiers from France, Britain, America, Canada, and Australia. They had many more troops than the Germans.

Instead of a loud bombardment to announce their plans, the Allies used a tactic called a "creeping barrage." This meant they moved forward while firing, which took the Germans completely by surprise. The French troops quickly broke through the enemy's defenses and captured important positions.

It was the first time tanks and soldiers worked together like this, and while there were some mix-ups, it worked well overall. By the end of the battle, only six tanks were still in action due to mechanical problems and losses, but the airplanes helped a lot by keeping the Germans off balance during the fight.

This time, General Haig made a smart choice. Instead of pushing for more fighting like before, he decided to pull back after just four days to prepare for a new attack. Ludendorff, the German general, saw this as one of the worst defeats for his army, calling it a "black day."

Because of this battle and the failure of the Spring Offensive, the German leaders realized they had lost the fight on the Western Front.

The Allies suffered around 44,000 casualties, while the Germans faced over 75,000 casualties, with 30,000 more surrendering during the battle.

This showed how much the Allies had improved their strategies and technology compared to the Battle of Frontiers four years earlier.

Battle of Megiddo

It's time to visit anther new area of fighting – Palestine!

The Ottoman Empire was using World War I to try to recapture lands it had lost during the Balkan Wars. Even though its army fought bravely in places like Gallipoli and other battles in the Mediterranean, they no longer had much control in the area.

When the British captured the city of Jerusalem at the end of 1917, it marked a turning point. The battle for Palestine became the Ottoman Empire's last chance to keep its power in the Middle East.

The Allies realized that if they could defeat the Ottomans there, it would be the end for them.

September 19–25

General Edmund Allenby had previously fought in the Boer War in South Africa, and now he had the important job of taking Palestine from the Turks. He was used to hot, dry weather, so he quickly adapted to the semi-desert conditions of the Middle East. Allenby understood how to mix new technology with soldiers, and this strategy worked well.

Instead of attacking the city of Gaza directly, Allenby decided to surround the enemy and capture Beersheba first. He cleverly tricked the Ottoman forces into thinking the British would attack from the east, while he launched his real assault from the desert.

The British bombarded the enemy just before the brave Australian Light Horse Brigade charged in, breaking through the defenses and opening the way to Gaza.

From that point on, the Turks were always on the run, retreating further and further. They even tried to counterattack at Megiddo, but Allenby had anticipated this move.

By combining air support, cavalry, artillery, and infantry, he trapped the enemy in a difficult situation. The defeated Ottoman Army surrendered, having lost 25,000 soldiers.

Coastal guns in Middle East, 1918

The rest of the region was easily taken as Allied forces moved through to Damascus. The Ottomans signed an armistice ending their role in the war, and effectively, their empire.

Meuse-Argonne Offensive

We're now fast approaching the final stages of WWI and one of the battles that brought the war to an end!

We're now back in Europe, where the Allies planned to push the Germans out of France and back behind the Hindenburg Line, on the German border.

This was a big offensive, and all the major countries were involved. The United States sent over one million soldiers to join the battle!

The Germans had been in control of this area for a long time, so they had built strong defenses. There were barbed wire fences, machine-gun positions, and concrete bunkers, which made it tough for the Allies to advance. They faced a lot of resistance as they tried to reclaim the land.

September 26–November 11

General Pershing, the leader of the US forces, began his attack early on the first day with a big three-hour bombardment of the enemy lines. The Americans quickly pushed through the first line of defenses, but their progress slowed down when German reinforcements arrived, and the rain made the Meuse River and Argonne Forests muddy and hard to fight in.

In October, the fighting became even more intense. The Allies kept pushing forward, but the Germans held their high ground and shot down at them. Instead of conducting one large attack, the Americans switched to smaller, surprise attacks to wear down the enemy before launching another big push. This was a new approach, different from the "Big Push" method that the British and French had been using in earlier battles.

On November 1st, the well-prepared Americans launched a strong advance, pushing the Germans back over 30 miles from their fortified positions. It was a great success!

However, the battle was very costly, with 26,000 American soldiers losing their lives and 120,000 more wounded, making it one of the deadliest battles in US history. Their efforts played a big role in breaking the German defenses.

The End of WW1!

At this stage, the Germans realised they were finished. After 4 years of intense fighting, it was running out of soldiers, food and supplies. Its

Spring Offensive had failed, and its soldiers were exhausted and even started refusing orders. Protests took place in Germany demanding an end to the war. The arrival of 1 million American soldiers and the success of the Allied advances made the German situation even worse.

Kaiser Wilhelm II was pressured to abdicate, and a new government was formed. The new leaders realized that continuing the war was hopeless, and they sought peace.

Just one week later, on November 11th, 1918, Germany signed the Armistice on Field Marshal Ferdinand Foch's personal train, ending the fighting at the **eleventh hour of the eleventh day of the eleventh month**.

Finally, after 4 years and 106 days, World War One was over!

Wall Street celebrates on the day Germany surrendered

13. LIFE IN THE TRENCHES

The western frontlines of Europe were a series of long, narrow trenches dug into the ground where soldiers could hide from enemy fire and to provide a safe place to stay while they waited for their turn to fight. Life in the trenches was very tough and challenging with disease, rats, and boredom a large part of life in the trenches!

Mud

The Western Front in France and Belgium was surrounded by forests and faced heavy rain in the spring and snow in the winter. These weather conditions made living in the trenches very tough, with tranches filling up with water after rain.

Even though pumps were used to try to remove the water, mud and wetness were always an issue. Finding a dry spot to sleep was almost impossible. Passchendaele was one of the worst places, where the water could rise up to the soldiers' waists! This made life very difficult, and many soldiers got a painful disease called trench foot.

Trench foot happens when your feet stay wet for too long. It can hurt a lot and can even damage the skin. The soldiers couldn't keep their feet dry, so they sometimes used whale oil to protect them. Despite all the challenges, the soldiers kept doing their best to support each other and carry on.

Stink

Before soldiers even stepped into the trenches, they could smell them! With so many tired and dirty men packed closely together, the muddy water, and even the smell of dead bodies nearby, it was really stinky.

The smell got even worse because the toilets, called latrines, were sometimes dug right in the trenches! Sometimes these toilets would overflow, which made the smell even more awful. To help with the stinky odors, workers would sprinkle things like chloride and lime around, but that sometimes made the smell even worse!

When new soldiers arrived at the trenches, many would feel sick from the terrible smells all around them.

Robert Graves describes what it was like:

"The smell was a compound of stagnant mud, latrine buckets, chloride of lime, unburied and half-buried corpses, rotting sandbags, stale human sweat, fumes of cordite and lyddite. Sometimes it was sweetened by cigarette smoke and the scent of bacon frying over wood fires, sometimes made sinister by the lingering odor of poison gas."

Highland Territorials in a WWI trench

Pests

It wasn't just soldiers who lived in the trenches. The muddy and unsanitary conditions attracted lots of animals. Some animals, like field mice and frogs, accidentally fell into the trenches and couldn't get out.

But the biggest problems came from rats and lice. With so many dead bodies around, the rats had plenty to eat, growing as big as cats! These pesky creatures spread disease quickly among the soldiers.

Lice were another problem. They crawled around and made the soldiers itchy and uncomfortable. After the war, doctors learned that lice helped cause something called "trench fever," which made the soldiers feel sick and gave them headaches.

Rations

Getting enough food for the two million soldiers on the frontlines was a really big challenge! Fresh vegetables were hard to find, so sometimes soldiers used weeds, leaves, and nettles to add flavor to their soups. By the time bread and biscuits arrived at the trenches, they were often stale and not very tasty!

Tommies eating in a trench

Cooking was another problem. Each battalion had two big pots to make food in, but they couldn't be washed properly every time. Soon, all the food started to taste the same! One of the most disliked meals was a canned soup called Machonochie. It was so bad that only very hungry soldiers would eat it.

When flour became hard to find in Europe, the cooks had to get creative. They started baking bread from dried potatoes, oats, barley, and sometimes even crushed straw!

To help hide the bad taste of the water, which had been stored in petrol cans and filtered with chemicals, most soldiers drank tea.

To make sure the enemy didn't know they were struggling, the British soldiers weren't allowed to complain about their food. They wanted to show the Germans that they were all happy and well-fed, even if that wasn't the truth!

- *DID YOU KNOW*
  - ***Soup powder and custard powder***, *as we have in shops today, were invented during World War 1 to make cooking easier and quicker on the frontlines.*

Routine

Unless they were involved in an attack, life in the trenches could become quite dull and repetitive. To keep the soldiers from getting too bored, they followed a schedule: four days in the trenches, four days in reserve, and four days resting. But the daily routine was mostly the same to maintain order on the frontlines.

- **Dawn:** Soldiers woke up early and got into their firing positions, ready for any enemy attacks. When their commander shouted, "Stand to!" it meant everyone had to be at their posts.

- **Daily:** Some soldiers, called sentries, had to keep watch, and an officer would check in on them every hour. No one could leave their post without permission, and they had to wear their full uniforms while on duty. At night or during foggy weather, they had to attach their bayonets to their rifles in case of surprise attacks.

Every day, the soldiers checked their rifles to make sure they were clean and free of mud or sand. They used an empty shell casing called a gas gong to warn everyone if there was a gas attack, so they could quickly put on their gas masks.

- **Night:** Supplies were brought into the trenches under the cover of darkness. The enemy knew this and often tried to attack the supply roads and tracks. Construction teams would come in to fix things like duckboards (raised wooden walkways), sandbags, and other equipment. Patrols would also go out at night to check for enemy listening posts or any weaknesses in their defenses.

Barracks built into the ground

The best way to get a small idea of what it was like in the trenches as a soldier is to read a bit from Rifleman William Eve's diary entry for January 7th, 1915:

> "Poured with rain all day and night. Water rose steadily till knee-deep when we had the order to retire to our trenches. Dropped blanket and fur coat in the water. Slipped down as getting up on parapet, got soaked up to my waist. Went sand-bag filling and then sewer guard for 2 hours. Had no dug out to sleep in... In one place we had to go through about 2 feet of water. Were sniped at a good bit... Roache shot while getting water and Tibbs shot while going to his aid. He laid in open all day, was brought in in the evening, unconscious but still alive. Passed away soon after."

Shell Shock

Soldiers who struggled to handle the stress of war were often seen as weak, and this was considered a punishable offense. Back then, people didn't understand that what we now call PTSD (Post-Traumatic Stress Disorder) was a real problem. Instead, they referred to it as "Shell Shock."

The war had changed a lot; the modern weapons and artillery were much louder, more dangerous, and fired more quickly than in previous wars. By the end of World War I, many soldiers showed similar signs of distress after experiencing the loud explosions of shells or witnessing terrifying attacks. It was a difficult time, and many heroes needed help that they didn't always receive.

The constant sound of war was all around as Robert Graves describes:

> "A German shell came over and then whoo - oo - ooooooOOO - bump - CRASH!... Rifle bullets in the open went hissing into the grass without much noise, but when we were in a trench the bullets, going over the hollow, made a tremendous crack. Bullets often struck the barbed wire in front of the trenches, which turned them and sent them spinning in a head-over-heels motion - ping! rockety-ockety-ockety-ockety into the woods behind."

Some soldiers experienced shaking, trembling, or trouble speaking. Others found themselves crying, having nightmares, or even sleep walking at night.

Doctors back then had a hard time understanding what these problems were and how to help. It's believed that about 80,000 cases of shellshock were officially recorded during the war, showing just how many men were affected by the stress of battle.

- ***DID YOU KNOW***

    - *Although life in the trenches was not nice, **9 out of 10 soldiers did survive** the trenches!*

14. WWI HEROES

Many brave soldiers did heroic things during the war, and their courage is still remembered today. Some risked their lives to save others, while others showed amazing bravery even when they were in danger. These soldiers weren't just fighting for their countries; they were also protecting their friends and fellow soldiers.

For example, some soldiers would leave the safety of their trenches to rescue injured friends, even while enemy fire was coming down on them. There were also pilots who flew in dangerous air battles, called dogfights, where they risked their lives to protect their side.

Nurses and medics were heroes too. They worked close to the fighting, helping injured soldiers and saving lives in tough and dangerous conditions.

Many people, both on the battlefield and behind the scenes, showed great courage during the war.

Their brave actions remind us of how strong and kind people can be, even in the hardest times.

During the war, there were different medals given to soldiers and civilians for their bravery. The most famous ones were awarded for incredible acts of courage:

- Great Britain awarded 633 Victoria Cross medals, its highest military honor.

- The US gave 126 Medals of Honor for "gallantry and bravery in combat at the risk of life above and beyond the call of duty." An extra 6 Medals of Honor were given to unknown soldiers from countries like Belgium, France, Great Britain, and Italy to remember those who had died.

- The War Cross, or Croix de Guerre, was the top French medal awarded to Allied soldiers who showed courage under fire.

- The Germans used the Iron Cross as a symbol of bravery during the war. You could see it painted on planes and military vehicles. It was given to soldiers who did amazing things in battle. But, as the war went on, the Germans started giving it out more often to try and lift people's spirits. By the end of the war, over 163,000 first-class Iron Crosses and 5 million second-class Iron Crosses were handed out. That means almost one in every three soldiers received one!

Let's look at some of these heroes and their stories.

Military

- **Sir Adrian Carton de Wiart**

Adrian Carton de Wiart was a remarkable soldier known for his incredible bravery. He fought in the Boer War, World War 1, and World War 2, and his adventures sound like stories from a legend! He wanted to be a soldier so much that he joined the fight in South Africa, even though he was too young and his father didn't want him to. While he was there, he got shot in the stomach and groin, which forced him to go back to England to heal. It took over ten years before he could return to being a soldier.

In 1914, during World War 1, de Wiart was serving with the Somaliland Camel Corps when he was shot again—this time in the face, which caused him to lose his left eye and part of his ear. Instead of taking a break, he threw away his glass eye and jumped back into battle! During the Second Battle of Ypres, he got hurt again when an explosion shattered his left hand. When the doctor didn't want to remove his injured fingers, de Wiart bravely pulled them off himself!

Even with just one eye and one hand, he didn't stop fighting. He led a group of soldiers at the Battle of the Somme in 1916, where he had to pull the pins from grenades with his teeth before throwing them at the enemy. His bravery earned him the Victoria Cross, the highest military award in Britain.

Later, during World War 2, de Wiart faced even more danger. When his plane was shot down, he swam to shore and tried several times to escape from a prisoner-of-war camp. Amazingly, after surviving so many close calls, he lived to be 83 years old. In his autobiography, he said, "Frankly, I had enjoyed the war," which shows just how tough and fearless he truly was!

- **Henry Johnson**

The "Harlem Hellfighters" was a special group of soldiers from the U.S. who were all Black. They served during a time when they didn't have the same rights as others in their country. Despite this, they bravely chose to fight in World War 1, taking part in some of the toughest battles on the Western Front.

One of their heroes was Henry Johnson. Before joining the unit, he worked as a railway baggage handler. He became famous for standing up to a whole group of enemy soldiers all by himself!

On the night of May 14, 1918, Johnson and his fellow soldier, Needham Roberts, were on guard in the trenches about 115 miles from Paris. They heard strange noises, so Johnson fired a flare into the sky to see what was happening. Suddenly, they saw a group of German soldiers charging toward them! Grenades began exploding, injuring both Johnson and Roberts. But instead of giving up, they fought back bravely.

Johnson fired his rifle at one soldier, but when it broke, he used it like a club to hit another! Even though he had been shot in the shoulder and leg, he fought off more soldiers with his knife. By the end of the battle, Johnson had 21 wounds, but he managed to scare away the entire group of 20 German soldiers, killing four of them all by himself!

His incredible courage made him a true hero, showing that bravery and determination can help overcome even the toughest challenges.

- **Alvin York**

Alvin York didn't want to go to war. His strong religious beliefs made him think that fighting was wrong, so he tried to avoid being drafted. But when his request was denied, he was sent to Europe as part of the American Army during World War 1.

On October 8, 1918, during the Meuse Argonne Offensive, York and his patrol were given a tough mission: to stop a German machine-gun battalion. As soon as they started, they were caught in heavy enemy fire, and many of his fellow soldiers, including his commander, were injured.

Instead of hiding, York stepped up and fought back alone. Because of his hunting skills, he was able to shoot quickly and accurately, taking down more than a dozen enemy soldiers. Some German soldiers tried to attack him, but York stopped them, too. Realizing they couldn't win, the German officer surrendered, and York took control of 90 prisoners!

As York led the captives back, he convinced even more German soldiers to give up. By the time he returned to the American lines, York had captured 132 prisoners all by himself! His bravery and quick thinking made him one of the greatest heroes of World War 1.

- **Edouard Izac**

Edouard Izac was born in Iowa, but his parents were from Germany, so he spoke German very well. This skill would help him when he joined World War 1. After graduating from the Naval Academy at age 25, Izac became a gunnery officer on a ship that carried American troops to Europe.

On May 31, 1918, his ship, the USS President Lincoln, was hit by three torpedoes from a German submarine (U-boat) and sank in less than 30 minutes. Izac was captured because he was one of the highest-ranking officers on board.

While he was on the U-boat, the German crew didn't know that Izac understood their language, so they talked freely around him. He learned a lot about the submarine's design, weapons, and plans. Knowing he had valuable information for the US, Izac made several daring escape attempts.

One of his wildest escape tries was jumping out of the window of a moving train! Even though he got hurt in the fall and was punished afterward, Izac never gave up. After months in different prison camps, he finally escaped in October 1918. He traveled 120 miles on foot, sneaking past guards and living off stolen vegetables until he reached Switzerland. There, he shared all the secret information he had gathered.

For his bravery, cleverness, and determination, Izac was awarded the Medal of Honor. He lived a long life and passed away at the age of 98 in 1990, making him the last living person to receive this special award for World War 1.

- **John 'Jack' Cornwell**

Jack Cornwell was just 16 years old when he became a hero at the Battle of Jutland during World War 1. Growing up in East London, Jack wasn't a star in sports or school, but he loved being a Boy Scout. He earned many badges for completing challenges, and with a father who had been a soldier, Jack was eager to serve his country. So, at age 15, he left school and joined the Royal Navy.

By February 1916, Jack had earned the rank of Boy First Class and was assigned to the HMS Chester, a British warship. His important job was to help aim the ship's 5.5-inch gun during battles, which was a dangerous position when under attack.

On May 31st, 1916, during the Battle of Jutland, Jack's ship was surrounded by four German cruisers. The enemy opened fire, hitting Jack's gun. Most of his crew were killed, and Jack was seriously injured by shrapnel in his leg and stomach. Even though he was hurt, Jack bravely stayed at his post for another hour, waiting for orders while the ship's captain steered them out of danger.

Sadly, Jack passed away from his injuries two days later, but his bravery was not forgotten. He was given a hero's burial, and later, the Boy Scouts created the Cornwell Badge to honor young people who showed courage and valor, just like Jack.

- **Georges Guynemer**

Georges Guynemer wanted to fight for France during World War 1, but when he tried to join the military, he was turned away because of health problems. Determined to help, he became a mechanic for the French Air Force. Eventually, he trained to be a pilot and joined an elite French squadron, flying powerful fighter planes.

Guynemer became a hero for his incredible flying skills and bravery, shooting down 53 enemy planes! But what made him truly respected in France was how he behaved in the air. In 1917, Guynemer faced one of Germany's best pilots, Ernst Udet, in an exciting dogfight. Both pilots twisted and turned through the sky, trying to outsmart each other. But during the fight, Udet's guns jammed, leaving him unable to fight back.

Instead of taking the easy shot, Guynemer showed great sportsmanship. He waved at Udet to signal that he wouldn't attack and then flew away, letting Udet live to fight another day.

Sadly, Guynemer's plane went down in battle on September 11, 1917, but he is remembered as a hero for both his skill and his honor in the air.

- **Flora Sandes**

Flora Sandes was the only British woman to become a soldier during World War 1. Unlike many women at the time, Flora loved adventure. She enjoyed shooting, riding horses, and even learned how to drive a car. When the war started, she traveled to Serbia to help as a nurse. But soon, she found herself right in the middle of the action!

One day, someone noticed how well she rode a horse and suggested that she become a soldier instead of a nurse. Flora agreed, took off her Red Cross nurse badge, and joined the Serbian army as a private. She became known as "Serbia's Joan of Arc" because of her bravery.

Flora fought on the front lines until she was injured by a grenade in 1916. While recovering, she was awarded the Serbian Order of the Kara-George, a special medal for bravery. By the end of the war, she had earned the rank of captain.

Flora Sandes once said, "People love to tell you that you can't do things," but she proved them wrong by becoming a courageous soldier!

- **Maria Bochkareva**

Maria Bochkareva grew up in a poor family in Russia and faced many challenges in her childhood. But she didn't let that stop her! Maria was determined to fight for her country, so she wrote a letter to the tsar (the Russian ruler) asking for permission to join the army. When she was allowed to enlist, she had to work hard to prove herself to the men in the army. She lived in the trenches, ate the same food as the soldiers, and bravely fought in battles, even getting injured a few times. Because of her courage, she earned several awards.

In 1917, Maria received an amazing honor—she was put in charge of her own unit called the "1st Battalion of Death," which consisted of 300 women she personally chose. These brave women were part of Russia's last attempt to fight against Germany.

However, when Russia's tsar, Nicholas II, was forced to step down and the Bolsheviks took over, Maria found herself in danger. She ended up being imprisoned for being on the wrong side of the revolution.

- **Heine von Heimburg**

Even though Germany lost the war, many soldiers showed great bravery. One such soldier was Heine von Heimburg, a German naval officer known for his daring escape on a submarine through a tricky waterway called the Dardanelles.

Heine was on the submarine U-22, named the Ocarina. The chances of getting through the Dardanelles without being spotted were very slim—only one in fifty! It was heavily guarded by British ships and artillery. When Heine saw British patrol boats, he had to quickly decide to dive underwater to avoid being seen.

However, the British had placed strong steel nets across the entrance. When the Ocarina got caught in the net, Heine couldn't submerge or back away without making things worse. The net snapped, alerting the British ships, which started firing at them. Instead of retreating, Heine made a bold choice and ordered the crew to go full speed ahead, pulling the net down with them. But the net jammed their motor, leaving them stuck and vulnerable while the British dropped bombs.

Finally, when night fell, Heine and his crew found no British ships around. Armed with hammers and hatchets, they cut the net loose and escaped into open water. Heine von Heimburg had successfully navigated through the Dardanelles, and for his bravery, he was awarded the German Order of Bravery!

- **Otto von der Linde**

Lieutenant Otto von der Linde was the youngest officer to receive the highest Prussian award, the "Pour le Mérite" medal for bravery, and he did something amazing - he captured a fort without firing a single shot!

Otto was part of the Fifth Guards marching through Belgium when they came across a strong fort called Fort Malonne, which blocked their way. The fort was surrounded by a wide open plain, making it dangerous to approach without heavy artillery. But Otto had a bold idea! He told his senior officers that he could take the fort with just four men. Even though it sounded a bit crazy, they decided to let him try.

Otto and his three brave friends marched across the open plain to the fort's gate. The Belgian commander looked down from the fort and listened as Otto bravely lied, saying there were big cannons hidden in the nearby forests ready to attack if they didn't surrender. The Belgian commander believed him! He opened the gate and ordered 25 soldiers to give up their weapons, while another 300 soldiers quickly escaped out the back!

After capturing the fort, Otto pulled down the Belgian flag and made a new German flag using black pants, a white shirt, and a red undershirt. Later, when a general rode by and asked who was in charge, Otto proudly introduced himself and his tiny army of four!

- **Sergeant Stubby**

This hero is a little different! During World War I, animals played important roles, helping soldiers with communication and transportation. Horses, mules, pigeons, and dogs were common, but very few received awards for their bravery. One special dog, Sergeant Stubby, a pit bull, earned many honors for his amazing deeds!

Stubby was part of the 102nd Infantry in the 26th Yankee Division. He belonged to Private Conroy and bravely served in 17 battles. Stubby was injured in a mustard gas attack, but afterward, he became an expert at detecting when the Germans used gas on the front lines. His incredible sense of hearing allowed him to warn soldiers about incoming artillery before they could even hear it themselves!

Stubby was not just a great soldier; he also comforted injured men waiting for help in a dangerous place called no-man's-land. One of his most famous moments was when he sniffed out a German spy hiding in the bushes! Stubby bravely pinned the spy down until American soldiers could come and take care of him.

Stubby survived many scary situations, including a grenade explosion. Because of his bravery, he was promoted to the rank of Sergeant and received many medals, even one from General Pershing! Sergeant Stubby was truly a hero, showing that dogs can be brave and loyal friends in times of war.

- **DID YOU KNOW**
    - *Henry Tandey was awarded the Victoria Cross in September 1918 for bravery in the Fifth Battle of Ypres and became the most decorated British private soldier in World War 1. However, he's remembered more for sparing Adolf Hitler's life in 1918, refusing to kill an unarmed soldier.*

Medical

- **Noel Chavasse**

Before he became a hero in World War I, Captain Chavasse was an Olympic athlete! He ran the 400-meters at the 1908 Olympics.

During the Battle of Ypres, Chavasse worked tirelessly for 15 hours, rescuing wounded soldiers. His bravery earned him the Military Cross. Later, at the Battle of the Somme, he saved 20 men even while he was injured himself and received his first Victoria Cross, which is a very special honor!

Captain Chavasse didn't stop helping others. He fought bravely at Passchendaele, going into no-man's-land again and again, even though he had a fractured skull! On August 4, 1916, a shell hit his first-aid post, injuring his face and stomach. Even after that, he tried to crawl for help but sadly passed away two days later. Because of his incredible bravery, he received another Victoria Cross, making him the only person to earn two of these awards in World War I.

Captain Chavasse's story reminds us of the courage and dedication of those who help others in times of danger!

- **Jane Jeffrey**

Jane Jeffrey was born in England but later moved to America, where she trained to become a nurse. When World War I began, she decided to go back to Europe to help by volunteering with the American Red Cross. She was stationed east of Paris, where conditions were very difficult.

On July 15th, 1918, something terrible happened. German airplanes attacked the hospital, dropping bombs that killed two people and injured 14 others, including Jane. It was very shocking because hospitals are meant to be safe places for doctors and nurses to help the wounded, and according to the Geneva Convention, it's not acceptable to attack them.

Even though she was severely injured, Jane remained to help others. This act of service gained her the French Legion of Honor award and the US Distinguished Service Cross.

- **Edith Cavell**

Edith Cavell was born in Britain and, was the head nurse at a hospital in Belgium, where she cared for soldiers who were hurt in the war. She always reminded her nurses to help anyone who came through the door, no matter which side they were on. In August 1914, when Germany invaded Belgium, she saw a chance to help British, Belgian, and French soldiers escape to safety in Holland.

Edith worked with a secret group to help over 200 men leave the hospital. They used an underground tunnel to sneak them out of the country. She made sure they had money, fake ID cards, and secret passwords so they wouldn't get caught. In fact, she even took 175 soldiers into her own home, hiding them until it was safe to escape!

However, the German police became suspicious about the disappearing soldiers and began watching the hospital closely. Friends urged Edith to leave Belgium for her safety, but she believed her work was too important. Sadly, on August 3rd, 1915, she was arrested when a spy discovered the underground tunnel beneath her hospital. Many people from different countries asked Germany to let her go, but she was executed by firing squad on October 12.

After the war, a big memorial service was held for Edith in London, and a statue was built near Trafalgar Square. Cavell is remembered as one of the pioneers of modern nursing, showing bravery and compassion in a time of great need.

- **Louise Thuliez**

Louise Thuliez was a French teacher living in a village that was taken over during the war. When she saw British soldiers who were hurt and left behind, she quickly helped them. This act of kindness led her to join the resistance, a group of people secretly fighting against the Germans.

In 1915, Louise teamed up with a brave nurse named Edith Cavell. Together, they helped smuggle wounded Allied soldiers to safety at Edith's house. But soon, the Germans noticed what they were doing, and Louise and Edith were caught.

At first, Louise was sentenced to death, but many people spoke up for her, and, unlike Edith Cavell, her punishment was changed to life in prison. After the war, Louise was awarded two special medals, the Legion d'Honneur and the Croix de Guerre, for her brave actions.

When World War II started, Louise once again helped smuggle Allied soldiers to safety. Her courage and determination to help others made her a true hero!

Communications

- **Grace Banker**

Telephones were very important for sending messages during the war, but regular soldiers often had a hard time with this job. So, General Pershing asked for volunteers to help operate the phones. A group of 223 women answered the call, and they became known as the "Hello Girls"!

Some of these brave women worked at headquarters, while others were stationed close to the front lines. A special team of 33 bilingual girls, led by Grace Banker, worked under tough conditions to connect important calls between the Allied forces. Grace kept a diary where she wrote about her experiences during the battles of St. Mihiel and Meuse-Argonne:

The cannons are roaring. 12 midnight. Capt. Scott, Miss Russell and myself went outside for a minute to look at the sky. There are great flashes of light all along the horizon like Northern Lights. 2:50am, the night railroad guns are beginning to roar... such a noise. Worse than a heavy surf in a storm. The old flimsy barracks shake and the beds rock as though in a miniature earthquake...

150,000 calls a day were connected by these switchboard operators. Their hard work and bravery helped keep communication open during the war, making a big difference for the soldiers on the front! For her role in the war, Banker received the Distinguished Service Medal.

- **Cher Ami**

During the war, sending messages was super important, and pigeons, dogs, and runners were used. During the Meuse-Argonne Offensive at the end of 1918, 442 pigeons were sent with messages!

A short note would be attached to the bird's leg in a small capsule. When the pigeon flew back to its coop, it would ring a bell to let the officer know a message had arrived.

One special pigeon named Cher Ami, "Dear Friend" in French, flew 12 important messages across the front lines in 1918. One of her most crucial missions was from Major Whittlesey, whose unit was surrounded by enemy troops. Out of 500 men, only 200 were left, and they desperately needed help!

Whittlesey had already sent a few pigeons to tell his commanders where he was, but the messages didn't get through. The enemy soldiers often shot at the birds, knowing they carried important information. To make things worse, the Americans accidentally fired artillery at their own men while trying to help!

Major Whittlesey sent Cher Ami, his last pigeon, with this message: "*We are along the road parallel to 276.4. Our own artillery is dropping a barrage directly on us. For heaven's sake, stop it.*"

The Germans opened fire as Cher Ami took off, but she flew 25 miles to deliver the note and helped save the 200 men!

Sadly, Cher Ami was injured during another mission and lost a leg. But she was so brave that General Pershing himself put her on a boat back to the United States! Cher Ami was awarded the French Croix de Guerre for her incredible bravery.

Spies

- **Marthe Cnoclaert**

Cnoclaert was training to be a doctor in Belgium when her country was invaded. Because of this, she had to work as a nurse in a hospital, caring for soldiers, but her heart always belonged to Belgium, not Germany. So when a British spymaster asked her to help, she was excited to join the war effort!

Her first mission was to gather information about Roulers Station, an important location for the German army's movements. Thanks to the details she provided, the Allies were able to successfully bomb the target in the spring of 1915!

While still working as a nurse, Cnoclaert was on duty when the first victims of a gas attack arrived. She worked tirelessly to care for them, and her dedication earned her the German Iron Cross as a recognition of her hard work. But when the Germans asked her to spy for them, she bravely refused!

In November 1916, Cnoclaert was arrested when the Germans became suspicious and set a trap for her. She had planted explosives near a German ammunition dump but accidentally left her watch behind, which had her initials on it. She was found guilty of spying and sentenced to death, but the head doctor spoke up for her, saying she had always been loyal to her country. Instead of being executed, she was sent to prison.

After the war, Cnoclaert was honored by the British, French, and Belgian armies, making her the only person to receive medals from all four major forces in World War I. Her bravery and commitment to her country were truly remarkable!

- **Gabrielle Petit**

Petit was very upset when the Germans invaded her country. She wanted to help fight back by gathering information to send to the Allies. She was invited to London to train as a spy, and after her training, she returned to Belgium to start her own spy network.

Petit traveled between France and Belgium, carefully delivering secret information about where the Germans were and what they were doing. Unfortunately, she was caught and arrested on January 20, 1916. The Germans interrogated her, but every time they did, she boldly told them how much she hated them for invading her homeland.

At her trial, she only spoke French and was sentenced to death by firing squad. It wasn't until after the war that people recognized her bravery as a spy. In May 1919, she was awarded the Croix de l'Ordre de Léopold for her courageous work.

Today, there is a statue in her honor at Place St Jean in Brussels, celebrating her bravery and dedication to her country!

- **Mata Hari**

Margaretha Zelle was born in the Netherlands and became an exotic dancer, taking on the name Mata Hari. She became very popular with wealthy and powerful men, including important government officials. Since the Netherlands stayed neutral during World War I, Mata Hari could travel freely between countries to meet her admirers.

Through her relationships, she picked up gossip and information, and both German and French spies approached her for help with the war. Whether she actually became a spy is still a mystery, but her actions made people suspicious. One of her admirers, a German Major named Arnold Kalle, sent a secret coded message, knowing the French would intercept it.

Mata Hari was arrested in Paris in February 1917, and five months later, she faced a closed trial. The French wanted to find someone to blame for their losses in the war and accused her of being a spy responsible for the deaths of many French soldiers. In July, she was taken before a firing squad and bravely refused to wear a blindfold.

Mata Hari died without anyone ever knowing the full truth about her involvement in the war.

15. HOW THE WAR CHANGED THE WORLD

World War I really changed the world and helped create the modern era. After the war, many nations and families were in mourning because so many soldiers had lost their lives. Old empires fell apart, which meant new maps were drawn and country borders changed.

Colonial countries started to seek independence from their rulers, and many people began to demand changes to the political systems that had been in place for a long time. In Russia, a big change called the Russian Revolution introduced a new idea called communism, while the United States began to emerge as an important power in the world.

These changes marked the beginning of a new age, full of new possibilities and challenges!

Let's take a look at some of these changes.

New Countries

After World War I, some big empires, like the Austro-Hungarian Empire and the Ottoman Empire, broke apart. This meant that new countries were formed, such as Czechoslovakia, Yugoslavia and Turkey. People had new borders to think about, and many nations became independent for the first time!

Changes in Leadership

Many kings and emperors lost their thrones because of the war. Countries started to be led by different types of governments, like democracies, where people could vote. For example, the Russian Empire turned into a country run by communists after the war.

Russia

Russia was the first country to go through a big change in leadership and politics. This change didn't happen because they lost the war like some other countries. Instead, many people were unhappy with Tsar Nicholas II and the wealthy upper class, which led to a revolution.

Many citizens didn't agree with the decision to go to war in the first place, and when the army suffered terrible defeats, workers and peasants decided to rebel. Tsar Nicholas II was not very popular, and his friendship with a mysterious man named Rasputin didn't help. While the rich lived in luxury, everyday people were struggling.

Vladimir Lenin, a young leader with new ideas, promised to make things better by giving power back to the people. After the Russian army's defeats at places like Tannenberg and Gorlice-Tarnow, it became clear that the war wasn't good for the country. This led to the Bolshevik Revolution, which changed everything.

Once Tsar Nicholas II was overthrown and killed, a new order began. Russia embraced communism, a political system that would be very significant in the world for the next 70 years, especially during World War II and the Cold War.

- *DID YOU KNOW*
    - *It was the **Germans who supplied the train** and its own soldiers to **transport Lenin into Russia** as part of their plan to help destabilize the country so that it would pull out of the war.*

Germany

Germany played a big part in starting the war and faced serious consequences. The Treaty of Versailles, which was signed after the war, made Germany give up some of the land it had controlled before. For example, it had to return Alsace-Lorraine to France and let Allied troops occupy the Rhineland.

Other places, like parts of Poland, Belgium, Denmark, and Russia, were also returned to their original countries. Interestingly, these were some of the first targets when Adolf Hitler began his campaign in World War II!

The German Empire lost 13% of its territory and had to give up its colonies. The Kaiser, who was the emperor, had to step down from his throne. A new government called a republic was created, but it was unstable. Different political groups began to fight for control, with some wanting to bring back the monarchy while others opposed the rise of communism.

It was during this confusing time, when the economy was struggling, that Adolf Hitler started to gain power.

Peace Treaties

Instead of bringing peace, what happened after World War I seemed to make things even worse. The countries that started the war had to face consequences for their actions, which led to the Treaty of Versailles. This treaty set strict rules for the Central Powers, especially Germany, but it didn't create peace; it made many people angry and hurt.

The treaty was created by the leaders of four Allied countries known as the "Big Four": Great Britain, France, the United States, and Italy. They decided on harsh punishments for Germany. Instead of using President Woodrow Wilson's ideas for peace, they focused on taking away land, reducing armies, and demanding Germany pay for the damage caused by the war. France's leader, Georges Clemenceau, insisted that Germany be punished as much as possible.

Rather than helping countries rebuild peacefully, the treaty made many people unhappy. The signing ceremony took place at the Palace of Versailles in France, and although many countries were there, only Britain, France, and America really made the important decisions.

Italy and Japan also fought in the war, but they didn't feel respected at the conference. They believed they weren't given the land they were promised, which made them feel left out. Leaders like Mussolini, Hitler, and Japanese generals used these feelings of anger and betrayal to gain power and ultimately to war again!

General Haig at Versailles

False Peace

After World War I, many new wars and struggles broke out in different countries, some even worse than the battles fought during the war. Following the Russian Revolution, there were arguments about borders, and many countries wanted to be independent.

These conflicts included the Finnish Civil War, which helped Finland become independent. The Estonian-Soviet War and the Latvian-Soviet War did the same for Estonia and Latvia. Poland also fought with Russia, Ukraine, and Lithuania to secure its borders. Greece battled against foreign forces, and both Ireland and Egypt wanted to free themselves from British control.

It wasn't until 1923 that things began to settle down and look more peaceful in the region. However, even though there was a calm on the surface, tensions and problems were still brewing underneath.

The League of Nations

The League of Nations was one of President Wilson's ideas to help countries work together and keep peace in the world. However, it didn't have much power because the United States, one of the strongest countries, decided not to join.

Without America's support, the League struggled to solve problems that arose after World War I. Countries like Germany, Japan, and Italy thought of it as a group of winners from the war and began to ignore its rules.

Social Changes

There were lots of changes in society, too! The upper class didn't have the same power and status as before. In countries like Russia, the upper class was challenged and broken apart to create a bigger working class under Communism. Similar changes happened in Germany when the kaiser had to step down, and the same occurred in Austria and Turkey.

Even in Britain, the class system was affected because many soldiers and officers from the upper class had died in the war. As a result, workers became a powerful group across Europe, with trade unions helping them get more rights and a bigger voice in politics and society.

One of the biggest changes was the role of women in society. While the men went off to fight in the war, women stepped up to take on jobs that were usually reserved for men. Instead of just staying at home to care for children, many women began working in factories. By 1918, one out of every ten workers making ammunition was a woman!

Because they were working in factories, many women stopped wearing dresses and corsets. Instead, they started to wear trousers and cut their hair short. A significant achievement for women in Britain was when some of them won the right to vote in February 1918, an important step toward equality.

Women working in a munitions factory

Advancements in Technology

Technological changes brought lots of exciting inventions that made life easier and faster! One of the biggest changes was the combustion engine, which helped create cars, tanks, airplanes, and powerful ships. But there were also important advancements in communication and medicine.

New ways to take photographs, record sounds, and communicate wirelessly became super helpful during the war and in everyday life. Instead of waiting for letters or newspapers, people could listen to the radio to get messages almost instantly. Governments could talk directly to their citizens no matter where they were. Movies were also used to lift spirits and keep everyone updated on what was happening.

In medicine, doctors were able to save many lives because of new advancements. They learned how to store blood, which helped keep patients alive. In 1917, a U.S. Army medic named Captain Oswald Robertson set up the first blood bank on the Western Front, and this idea later saved many lives in hospitals. A special device called the Thomas Splint was created to help soldiers with broken legs. Before this invention, four out of five soldiers with broken legs would die, but after it was used, four out of five survived!

Other medical advances included screenings for tuberculosis, treatments for tetanus, vaccines for typhoid, and ways to prevent infections during surgeries. All these new inventions and methods didn't just help during the war—they also made life better for everyday people. The world was becoming more connected and modern than ever before!

Economic Changes

The balance of power between nations began to shift economically, meaning that some countries became stronger while others struggled, particularly as European countries had to rebuild after the war.

It cost millions of dollars to train, equip, and feed entire armies and to create new weapons. By 1918, just one day's worth of bullets cost around £3.8 million (or about $4.5 million)!

It's no wonder that countries like Britain had to take out loans to pay for the war. The problem came afterward when they had to start paying back those loans. With food shortages and other resource problems, this added financial strain was really tough.

In France, many workers were affected because over one million soldiers returned home disabled and couldn't work. The war had also destroyed a lot of farmland and damaged important roads, bridges, and buildings.

- **DID YOU KNOW**

    - *Despite more than 100 years passing since the war, farmers in France and Belgium still uncover over **900 tons of unexploded WW1 artillery shells each year**!*

Germany faced even tougher challenges. The Treaty of Versailles required Germany to pay a whopping £6,600 million (which is about £284 billion today) in damages for what they caused during the war.

By 1923, with hyperinflation, their money was almost worthless, and they couldn't pay back the debts they owed. This made things really hard for them and contributed to the rise of Adolf Hitler, who decided to go against the Western powers.

Most countries struggled to recover and had to deal with the double impact of the Great Depression in the 1920s and the financial crash of 1929. This created a lot of tension and anger between nations.

The only country that came out ahead was the United States. Since it had joined the war later and its economy wasn't as badly affected as Europe's, it became the leading financial power in the world and the main bank for other countries.

- **DID YOU KNOW**

    - *It took almost **100 years for the UK to finish paying its £7 billion ($8.4 billion) debt for World War 1**, making its last instalment in 2015*

    - *In **2010, Germany paid back all its loans** used to make reparations.*

- *If dealing with the 20 million deaths from WW1 was not enough, after all the fighting there was more to come. This time it was a pandemic called the **Spanish Flu** (it probably originated somewhere else, but because it was reported in newspapers in Spain first, the name stuck!)*

The movement of troops helped to spread it quickly across Europe as soldiers were housed together for long periods. By the summer, Russia, Africa, Asia, and New Zealand all had cases.

*It's thought that between **50-100 million died from the epidemic** —(3 to 5% of the entire World population!) more than the deaths from WW1.*

Remembering the Fallen

War memorial in Somme, France

Every year, people around the world remember those who died fighting for their country and standing up for what they believed in. Armistice Day marks the end of World War I on November 11th. The first time it was remembered was in Britain in 1919, when people observed two minutes of silence at 11 a.m. Soon, other countries in the Commonwealth followed this tradition, making it an important day on the calendar.

In Britain, the red poppy became a symbol of remembrance because it was one of the few flowers that bloomed in the Flanders region of Belgium, where the fighting had destroyed everything else.

- **DID YOU KNOW**
  - *After World War II, Armistice Day was changed to **Remembrance Day** to honor those who lost their lives in that war as well.*
  - *In the United States, November 11th is called **Veterans Day***
  - *On **May 9th, Russia honors its soldiers from World War II** instead of focusing on World War I.*
  - *In Germany, remembering the soldiers from either war can be difficult since they were on the losing side, so they hold a **national day of mourning** that is more low-key compared to Remembrance Day or Veterans Day.*

After the war, Britain and France hurried to build large statues and plaques to honor those who died. This led to some impressive memorials that still stand today.

Tyne Cot War Graves near Passchendaele

One important monument in the UK is the Cenotaph, in Whitehall, London. Built in 1920, it is a tribute to all the families who lost loved ones in World War I. Most soldiers were buried close to where they fell, so the Cenotaph symbolizes their absence and is a central place for public mourning.

- **DID YOU KNOW**

  ○ *The word "Cenotaph" means* ***"empty tomb"*** *in Greek.*

In Hyde Park, you can find the Royal Artillery Memorial and the Machine Gun Corps Memorial, while the Field Marshal Earl Haig Memorial and the Edith Cavell Memorial are in other parts of London.

France also has many memorials, including six villages that were never rebuilt after being destroyed during the war. These villages serve as reminders of the devastation and have mayors who help take care of them and ensure that any soldiers' remains found are identified and properly buried.

In Britain, France, and America, there are tombs dedicated to unknown soldiers. People gather each year on November 11th at Westminster Abbey in London, the Arc de Triomphe in Paris, and Arlington National Cemetery in Virginia to remember those who fought and died for their countries.

- *DID YOU KNOW*
    - *The Menin Gate near Ypres is one of the only monuments that **removes names!** With over **55,000 names of those who have no known grave**, a name is only removed when the remains of a soldier are found and identified*
    - *"**Thankful villages**" are the **53 villages** in Britain out of 16,000 **which lost no men in WW1**, because all those that served came home. Unlike most other villages, these don't have war memorials to commemorate the dead.*

16. CONCLUSION

> *"Those that fail to learn from history, are doomed to repeat it"* – Winston Churchill

Looking back at history helps us understand what could have been done better. That's why people say, **"It's always easier in hindsight."**

It's easy for us now to see how wrong it was to lose 20 million lives over one archduke. We can criticize leaders like General Haig, who sent thousands of soldiers into battles that didn't seem to change anything. At the time, though, those decisions might have seemed like good ideas based on what had worked in the past.

World War I was a confusing and messy time. What many thought would be a quick war turned into years of fighting with no clear winner. The war changed rapidly, with new technology and ideas emerging as old methods were discarded. It was a tough birth for the modern age, especially on the Western Front.

Many generals made poor choices at the beginning of the war, which led to unnecessary loss of life. But by 1918, they learned from their mistakes and started using better strategies that combined technology with soldiers. They benefited from hindsight, understanding that old tactics weren't working anymore.

History is all about learning from the errors of others so we don't repeat them. After WWI, everyone hoped it would be the last war, wanting to avoid making the same mistakes. But history can be like a loop, and sometimes things happen again!

The Treaty of Versailles was supposed to bring peace but ended up creating new problems that led to more fighting, and World War II. To truly stop fighting, we need to learn from the past and find better ways to resolve our differences. By studying WWI, we can see the importance of finding peaceful solutions to avoid future conflicts.

Thank you for joining me on this journey through WW1. I'm glad we made it through safely!

If you enjoyed this trip through WWI, remember there are always more adventures to explore! Look out for more books at james-burrows.com.

If you enjoyed this book, I would be really grateful if you could share your thoughts in a review on Amazon. Thank you!

ABOUT THE AUTHOR

James is a military and history expert, developing an early interest in military history from stories told by his grandfathers, one of whom was a POW spending 4 years in a camp in Poland, and even his great-grandfather, who fought at the Somme.

Whether writing about WW2, Greek Mythology, Roman Emperors or Alexander the Great, James hopes to spark a healthy curiosity and love for history in today's young people.

When not working or spending time with his wife and children, James can be found walking his two beautiful black labradors in the local countryside, pondering ideas for his next book.

See more at: james-burrows.com

www.ingramcontent.com/pod-product-compliance
Lightning Source LLC
Chambersburg PA
CBHW072054110526
44590CB00018B/3164